Living a Life of Significance

Joseph W. Jordan

The American College Press

MetLife®

The American College

The American College® is an independent, nonprofit, accredited institution founded in 1927 that offers professional certification and graduate-degree distance education to men and women seeking career growth in financial services.

The Center for Financial Advisor Education at The American College offers both the LUTCF and the Financial Services Specialist (FSS) professional designations to introduce students in a classroom environment to the technical side of financial services, while at the same time providing them with the requisite sales-training skills.

The Solomon S. Huebner School® of The American College administers the Chartered Life Underwriter (CLU®); the Chartered Financial Consultant (ChFC®); the Chartered Advisor for Senior Living (CASL®); the Registered Health Underwriter (RHU®); the Registered Employee Benefits Consultant (REBC®); and the Chartered Leadership Fellow® (CLF®) professional designation programs. In addition, the Huebner School also administers The College's CFP Board—registered education program for those individuals interested in pursuing CFP® certification, the CFP® Certification Curriculum.

The Richard D. Irwin Graduate School® of The American College offers the master of science in financial services (MSFS) degree, the Graduate Financial Planning Track (another CFP Board-registered education program), and several graduate-level certificates that concentrate on specific subject areas. It also offers the Chartered Advisor in Philanthropy (CAP®) and the master of science in management (MSM), a one-year program with an emphasis in leadership. The National Association of Estate Planners & Councils has named The College as the provider of the education required to earn its prestigious AEP designation.

The American College is accredited by **The Middle States Commission on Higher Education**, 3624 Market Street, Philadelphia, PA 19104 at telephone number 267.284.5000.

The Middle States Commission on Higher Education is a regional accrediting agency recognized by the U.S. Secretary of Education and the Commission on Recognition of Postsecondary Accreditation. Middle States accreditation is an expression of confidence in an institution's mission and goals, performance, and resources. It attests that in the judgment of the Commission on Higher Education, based on the results of an internal institutional self-study and an evaluation by a team of outside peer observers assigned by the Commission, an institution is guided by well-defined and appropriate goals; that it has established conditions and procedures under which its goals can be realized; that it is accomplishing them substantially; that it is so organized, staffed, and supported that it can be expected to continue to do so; and that it meets the standards of the Middle States Association. The American College has been accredited since 1978.

The American College does not discriminate on the basis of race, religion, sex, handicap, or national and ethnic origin in its admissions policies, educational programs and activities, or employment policies.

The American College is located at 270 S. Bryn Mawr Avenue, Bryn Mawr, PA 19010. The toll-free number of the Office of Professional Education is (888) AMERCOL (263-7265); the fax number is (610) 526-1465; and the home page address is theamericancollege.edu.

Dedication

In memory of my mom—

whose spirit and dedication has led me to live a life of significance.

CONTENTS

Acknowledgments

The author wishes to express sincere appreciation to his wife, Geraldine; his daughter, Sarah; and his son, Joey for their support and encouragement.

Gratitude goes to the those who shared their stories in the book: Jack Dempsey, T.J. Rogers, Ann Marie Miller, Art Steinberg, Bob Weaver, Paris Lewis, Lonnie Colson, Mike Amine, Ying Ling Zhang, and Roland Basinski.

Special thanks to Joel L. Franks, whose dedication and perseverance has made this book possible.

About the Author

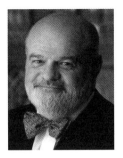

Joseph W. Jordan, Senior Vice President of MetLife, is an industry-renowned thought leader in the areas of behavioral finance, client-centric tools, ethical selling and client advocacy. He helps financial professionals around the world recognize and celebrate the intrinsic value that they deliver to their clients. He is also a well-respected speaker who is famous for his inspirational messages.

Joe started his career with Home Life in 1974—was named "Rookie of the Year" and became a member of Million Dollar Round Table (MDRT) the following year. He ran insurance sales at Paine Webber from 1981–1988. He joined MetLife in 1988 to manage annuity (and later life) sales and product development. He is currently responsible for

MetLife's Behavioral Finance Strategies

Joe was a main platform speaker at the 2004 MDRT Conference as well as the 2006 and 2010 MDRT Experience in Bangkok, Thailand and Seoul, Korea. He was a main platform speaker at GAMA's Leadership and Management Program (LAMP) Conference (in 2006 and 2009), In 2008, Joe was the keynote speaker at LIMRA's Retirement Industry Conference as well as the keynote speaker at MDRT Ireland, Greece and Poland between 2009 and 2010. Joe is also a founder of the Insured Retirement Institute (formally known as the National Association of Variable Annuities, or NAVA). In 2010, he was selected as one of the top 50 Irish Americans on Wall Street.

Joe is married with two children, lives in Manhattan and is a member of the Fordham University Football Hall of Fame. He also played rugby for over 30 years with the New York Athletic Club.

Introduction

It's not easy being an insurance man or woman in today's world. You face rejection on a daily basis. You talk about a topic that no one wants to talk about. You are working in one of the most challenging economic environments ever witnessed in our lifetime. But it's also a time for unprecedented opportunity to not only make a great living, but to make a significant impact on your clients and the people that depend on them. As in the introduction of Charles Dickens's novel, *A Tale of Two Cities*: "It was the best of times, it was the worst of times...."

You could have chosen any other career path—but you didn't. You might have entered the business with the intent of making a truckload of money, but as you might have already discovered, there is a more profound journey that awaits you. Joe Jordan knows how to keep you inspired, to help you overcome the daily challenges you face. He knows from personal experience. He knows what it takes to be a real hero.

Reflecting on his early childhood life and business experiences, Joe has come upon several revelations he wants to share with you about the questions all of us face in the course of our lives. Whether you are a young person, choosing a first step on your career path, or a seasoned veteran surveying a life's work, Joe's insights can help you understand what it is to *live a life of significance.*

As we emerge from the "Information Age," we have come to realize that the answers to questions about the significance of life do not lie in facts or data alone. They lie in inner resources we cannot always name, resources that guide us in those moments when the facts tell us something is impossible. At these moments, we connect with the things that make us truly human, not just in an emotional sense, but in the scientific sense as well. As scientists delve deeper into genetic research, the attributes that they have identified as uniquely human seem to dwell in our ability to have empathy for others, to understand what we may know about their situations that they do not, and to be able to provide solutions to educate them and improve their lives.

Through your chosen profession you have a unique opportunity to go beyond a feeling of empathy and to bring about positive results not only in the lives of people you know, but those you may never meet—the children and grandchildren of your clients. When you protect the well-being of another person, you have done something deeply and profoundly human—in the best sense of the word. When you return to that person in the moment when your advice has delivered on its promise, you have known what it is to live a life of significance.

In this book, Joe Jordan will connect the dots of just such a life, from its earliest beginnings to today, with guiding principles for the future. Drawing on three decades of personal and professional growth and reaching back into the early life experiences that set him on his path, Joe Jordan will help you gain a foothold on the road to significance by revealing his own journey. Through this journey, you may come to see yourself differently and find yourself better equipped to take your next step toward even greater meaning.

I.

Do You Hear What I Hear?

"The important thing is not to stop questioning. Curiosity has its own reason for existing. One cannot help but be in awe when one contemplates the mysteries of eternity, of life, of the marvelous structure of reality. It is enough if one tries merely to comprehend a little of this mystery every day. Never lose a holy curiosity."

— Albert Einstein

Sometimes in our society, we believe we are not supposed to question our choices in life—particularly in our professional lives. We worry that questioning is a sign of weakness, or worse, we are afraid of where the questions might lead us. But when we question, we are actually in good company. I can say that now with utter confidence. And I can tell you, I didn't always realize it. If I can help one person see the value of that "holy curiosity" that Einstein spoke of, I feel that I will have shared a valuable lesson.

To help inspire the practice of questioning, you'll find prompts from time to time offset from the text of the book.

As I write this book, global markets are still reeling in the wake of Wall Street's 2008 financial crisis, commonly known as The Great Recession. But I don't want to start the conversation there. With more than thirty years in the industry at my disposal, I want to draw more deeply from the reservoirs of experience and recast today's challenges in the context of patterns that transcend the details of the current situation. Patterns of human behavior and natural law reach back through history and will continue to shape human history well into the future. Recognizing patterns in your own life can help you cultivate the skills you need to ensure that your personal history will reveal a life of significance.

In the early 1990s, I joined MetLife after almost a decade on Wall Street. At the time, brokers and insurance agents were operating in two distinct cultures, with two different approaches to their clients. I was coming from Paine Webber's asset-gathering broker culture. My role at MetLife was to focus on building its annuity business. That business existed within a culture of protection-focused life insurance agents whose goal was to gather income. Looking back, I suspect that I was hired primarily because of my extensive knowledge of the product. But, from my perspective, the most important knowledge I brought with me was an understanding that human behavior in the context of industry culture has everything to do with the sales process. I instinctively knew that the brokerage and insurance industries had different cultures and what I ultimately had to do was not train people on a product, but to alter their behavior.

Back in the investment world, brokers focus on accumulation of assets in investment portfolios. Depending on the broker and the client, the amount of a single transaction could vary greatly. If a client had a million dollars in assets to invest, a broker would be interested in bringing as much of that million under management as possible. Having been in the life insurance business, I understood that for the most part, life insurance people gathered income for protection purposes. They never asked for a million dollars up front. In terms of behavior, that was the fundamental difference between the two.

What was not discussed much in the 1990s was the fact that all financial products are tied on some level to human needs and desires. The key for me ultimately would be to find the connections between the cultures that ruled Wall Street and those that fueled the insurance industry and to leverage both to the advantage of the protection product marketplace.

In my early years at MetLife, we began to recognize that the best route to asset-gathering in the insurance culture would be to become a viable provider of financial planning services. Fee-based financial planning had been emerging for some time, as traditional barriers between brokerage, banking, and credit were lifted by legislation, and a more fluid financial services industry was born. In this fluid environment, an institution like MetLife with traditional roots in insurance products had an increased capacity to provide a wide range of products and services to its clients. A financial planning model would allow us to aggregate those products and services within the context of a client's individualized plan. But it would not happen overnight.

I can see myself standing at the window of my office on an autumn day in 1998, just a few years after coming to MetLife. I was grappling with a nagging question: Why wasn't the financial planning business soaring? But I wasn't sure why I was asking it. All in all, things were good. Our financial planning approach at MetLife—then in its infancy—was gaining momentum; sales figures were good. It was the height of the Information Age, and our "information" was giving us a pretty positive picture. I just had the sense that something was holding both the planners and the clients back from understanding the full potential of the process. I was wondering whether there was something wrong with the process itself. But I would come to realize that was not the issue.

By that time, I had spent twenty-five years in the financial industry, and I had seen a lot of changes. I had been on the insurance side of the investment business and the investment side of the insurance business. I had charted my career as an "outlier."[1] I always liked coming from the outside into a new situation, bringing expertise from another industry or experience into the mix for the industry I joined. From this vantage point, I had enjoyed a fairly unique perspective on the changes in finance that had taken place in the final third of the 20th Century.

On this day in the late 90s, I was wrestling with two questions related to financial planning—one about clients and one about planners. From the client perspective, I wondered, "If people are armed with the information they need to plan a solid financial future, why are they slow to put the plan into action?" I knew that financial planning made inherently good sense. Our clients understood the value of a plan—at least to the extent that they would purchase the plan itself. But they were not as engaged when it came to following the advice the plan laid out for them. From the planner's perspective, I wondered what was preventing them from embracing the planning model wholeheartedly. This is why I wondered if the process itself needed fixing. At the time, the root of my concern was not yet clear to me. Ultimately, I would discover that these two questions were tied to a single common denominator: behavior. But, at the time all I had was a hunch about some of the issues at play.

---

1.   Malcolm Gladwell

"Intellectual awareness and knowledge of something motivates us to do nothing."

— David Hume

THAT TIME BEFORE

When I started in the insurance business in 1974 at a small company called Home Life (now Phoenix Home Life), everyone was selling products that had been around for many years: whole life and term life. It's important to remember that in the 1970s, insurance, banking, credit, and investing operated separately from one another. Most working Americans, if they had anything they called a retirement account, would have had a pension or some other defined benefit plan for retirement. Most (although more men than women in those days) also had some form of traditional life insurance. There was no motivation to design updated insurance products at that time.

As the 70s gave way to the 80s, however, America was facing record inflation and an oil crisis, compounded by the hostage crisis in Iran, which made Americans feel vulnerable in ways we hadn't for generations. Products like life insurance policies that relied on cash values with fixed interest rates (even healthy ones) suddenly seemed doomed to be outpaced by inflation. (Interestingly, history shows that the majority of the whole life policies held by policyholders through that time period performed quite well.)

By 1980, changes had begun that would ultimately break down the walls dividing the different categories of financial institutions. By the mid-80s, defined-benefit plans (like the pensions I mentioned above) had been largely replaced by defined contribution plans. Most working people had a 401(k), and market-based investing—once the pursuit of sophisticated institutional investors—now reached a new, and mostly uninitiated audience of "investors." Everyone from the proverbial kid in the mailroom to the CEO in the executive suite had a more immediate stake in the markets.

The allure of the investment culture was compelling. Choice and control were the bywords of the day. People saw personal investing as a way to increase their chances of earning higher returns on their money than traditional savings accounts along with

16

hands-on control of how their assets were allocated. If the appeal of a defined benefit plan was the security of knowing the amount you would receive in retirement, the appeal of the defined contribution plan was the potential to earn more by controlling the underlying investments directly. With inflation threatening to diminish future dollar values, the marketing story of the defined contribution was quite effective. From the employer's perspective, the appeal was in shifting the fiscal responsibility onto employees and alleviating a growing financial burden for what would ultimately be America's largest group of retirees, the Baby Boomers.

A powerful current swept people toward Wall Street. Not only did the appeal of investing grip the public, the appeal of investment careers called to the big crop of "twenty-somethings" with business training and energy to pursue their goals. Along with two friends, I decided to dive into the "cool" end of the financial services pool by joining a boutique investment firm as their resident insurance expert.

At the time, the product at the intersection of investing and insurance was the annuity. Annuities, like most products at that time, were fairly straightforward in their design. As a guaranteed income vehicle, a vanilla annuity product could be described as upside down life insurance. While life insurance paid benefits for those who died prematurely based on a mortality pool by those who lived longer, annuities paid income for those who lived longer into retirement age funded by the resources left by those who did not. That was the premise.

However, the design premise and the sales strategy did not always match. Annuities were soon being sold by brokerage firms as tax-deferred investments. With interest rates hovering around 15%, and equities at a low ebb, brokers took notice. Soon brokers discovered that their clients could take money out, on a FIFO basis, which means first in, first out. These annuities were being sold like ten-year tax-free municipal bonds. (Since they were allowed to withdraw at least 10% of their investment each year, they would have tax free income for the first 10 years. (At the time, annuities allowed people to withdraw basis or principle first. Later this was changed to LIFO, which is last in, first out—making the withdrawal taxable.) Another interesting wrinkle I discovered was that, for the most part, the annuity products our company was selling came from small, lesser-known insurance companies. These companies could offer high interest rates because they were not carrying the huge bond portfolios that the big insurers had at the time backing their existing life policies.

Also large, established life insurance companies had a protection income-gathering culture and were late to enter this use of annuities. At this point, on the insurance side of the aisle, the need to update insurance products began to seem more pressing.

I realized, looking back, that the same questions were tugging at me back then that I am focused on today: What will help people make the right choices for a lifetime and for the generations to follow them? I understood the value of an insurance policy or an annuity when purchased with the appropriate goals in mind. As I watched the way the protection benefit of the annuity was being downplayed or ignored in the sales conversation, even then, I had questions *not* about the products, but about how they were being sold. When you ask a product to perform in a way other than it was designed to perform, what new risks are you introducing? I wondered. It seemed to me that no one was looking at the products holistically.

Not everyone on Wall Street in the 80s had this question in their minds. I'm sure that I couldn't have articulated the relevance of my questions at the time either. But I came to realize fairly quickly that when products are bought and sold for reasons other than those for which they were structured, problems follow. Even in my twenties, I did not feel comfortable with this practice. But, I did not yet have the benefit of experience that would help me understand the source of my discomfort.

So when my friend John Moran, who had taken the plunge into the Wall Street waters with me, came into my office and told me that Paine Webber was looking for someone to run the insurance department I was glad for a chance to move on. I was not immune to the stigma that insurance agents were feeling during this period, and I wanted to change my image. It didn't hurt either that Paine Webber was a major broker-dealer at the time with an excellent reputation. At first, to be honest, I was completely intimidated at the prospect of heading a department there—even in my field. But, when John said, "Joe, just go to the interview," I went.

When have you done something despite feeling intimidated?

I think most people can relate when I say that I went into that interview feeling both less qualified and more qualified than I actually may have been. When we started the interview, I had no

18

way of knowing what I might be asked. But as the questions came, my confidence rose. I began to realize that despite the interviewer's seniority, I really did have expertise that he did not have.

"Tell me about Section 264." Something in the way he asked this question tipped me off to the fact that I knew more than he did about how to answer.

"Sure. That's the minimum deposit requirement that allows the efficient purchase of life insurance by paying the first four years of the seven-year premium up front." You see, the policy that Paine Webber had in mind was a high cash value, low death benefit plan. For example, a premium of $10,000 gave you an initial death benefit of $14,000 after which you pay four out of seven years and then borrow the full cash value out while continuing to deduct interest. Future premium payments were paid for by loans which were tax deductible offset by tax-free withdrawals of excess cash from the policies. The result was predictable, multiple write off.

You might wonder who would buy a $14,000 life insurance policy for $10,000. At that time there was no standardized definition of life insurance. So creative minds set out to create products that if considered life insurance assured considerable tax benefits. This was not insurance, this was a tax shelter. What was being manipulated were the tax advantages life insurance enjoyed as a social good. When the deductibility of interest and the proper definition of life insurance was legislated, this program died.

I could see that the answer had struck a chord. The next question came quickly. "Can you do this job?"

"Of course I can." I heard myself saying. And somewhere inside I knew that I could… or I might fail... but it was a risk worth taking.

"Then it's yours."

National Sales Manager for insurance products at Paine Webber, in charge of 4,300 brokers. I gave notice to John Moran with his blessings and he wished me luck. My wife helped me pick out a couple of new suits. Then I rolled up my sleeves and went to work.

My top priority was to get acquainted with all the brokers and all the suppliers who worked with us. It meant a grueling travel schedule and long hours, but I learned a great deal in short order including all the ins and outs of booking airline tickets and filing travel expenses! It was all new to me. What I already knew were the products. In the 80s, insurance was—as I said before—often used for tax purposes in the investment world.

I had come to Paine Webber primarily because I wanted to be "cool." But Paine Webber also gave me the chance to be affiliated with a substantial, reputable firm. The firm's reputation was reassuring, not only to clients, but to those of us who worked there in these times of rapid-fire changes. The markets and products were evolving quickly. The demand for returns and performance drove everything the insurance companies were designing. I had an instinctual sense that there would need to be a broader context for investors to remain secure. To achieve this, I worked with brokers to make them more comfortable selling annuities, since they would be able to gauge how these products would fit in a client's portfolio. At the same time, I worked to involve life insurance experts in selling investments, again providing a broader perspective on how their products would fit into the larger financial picture for a client.

Of course, by the 80s no one wanted to be identified as a life insurance agent. Everyone who wasn't a registered broker wanted a title like financial advisor or investment representative. Once again, it would take years for me to recognize the discomfort this raised for me at the time. I knew that it was unhealthy for people to feel that they had to hide their profession. But at the time I didn't think about the additional layer of confusion this attitude added to a market where products were being sold as something other than what they were intended to be. And I was years away from realizing how this basic self-esteem issue could affect sales overall.

Another phenomenon of this era was the junk bond. Michael Milken built a junk bond empire on the illusion created by massive liquidity, high coupon rates, and timing. People were lulled into enjoying these bonds without realizing the high risk of their underlying investments. Ultimately, of course, the illusion was dispelled, the junk bonds collapsed, and Milken went to jail for fraud.

An article about a company called Executive Life, which appeared in *Fortune* and on CNN.com in 1992, highlights the issues that were affecting the less stable parts of insurance industry in some of its early attempts to sell protection products based on performance numbers. The gist of it was grabbing for growth with insufficient assets to underwrite the risk and causing outside auditors to raise the alarm. It was a poisonous cocktail for Executive Life's Fred Carr and his investors.

From my position within Paine Webber, I could see the changes happening before my eyes. The bellwether case of undercapitalized annuity risk was Baldwin-United which was mentioned in the same article. Baldwin's story unfolded in the early 80s and illustrates the pitfalls that lay in the path of products and companies that were manipulated for "unnatural purposes." Baldwin was a successful piano company run by Morley Thompson. Thompson was inspired by another 80s Wall Street trend: creating corporate conglomerates. A company, regardless of its traditional focus (for example, in Baldwin's case, pianos—talk about a culture disconnect) could acquire businesses across industries to realize profits from a number of sectors. Thompson decided to parlay his piano business into a multifaceted financial services concern. Thompson acquired small insurance companies and began offering annuity products. Unencumbered by large low interest rate bond portfolios and able to offer double-digit interest rates packaged within the apparent safety of an insurance company, the plan was initially successful.

Thompson's fatal error was to invest the money Baldwin United was raising with these products in "affiliated assets," which is to say, all the money was funneled back into building the corporation to keep building the conglomerate. Actuarial firms and rating agencies were not equipped to assess the security of these types of cobbled-together corporate structures. But the rumors began flying that Baldwin United was unstable.

When the tremors reached those of us in the brokerage community, there was a range of reactions. One highly qualified actuary from a prestigious firm tried to calm my fears. I finally asked him point-blank, "If your mother owned one of these policies, would you tell her to stay in?"

"Most certainly," he insisted. But I never got to ask him how he felt about his mother.

A colleague at another Wall Street firm confided that he was going to advise his clients to take out half of the funds in their Baldwin United annuities. To which I shot back, "Which half? The good half or the bad half?" No one wanted to create a run on the bank. But my own internal conversation was bubbling over. At home, with family and friends, anywhere I could get someone to listen, I was full of anxiety and endless information about insurance commissioners and actuarial assessments. People started to dread the headline or random comment that would send me off on these "inside baseball" conversations.

In the midst of this brewing storm, Paine Webber flew us to Club Med for a brokers' meeting. It was my first trip to an island resort. But, from the moment we stepped from the plane and saw the crystal waters and white sand beaches, I somehow knew that I would not be able to stay and enjoy myself.

Sure enough, the storm broke—literally and figuratively. As the dark clouds rolled in from the ocean, and rain started teeming down on the veranda, word came from New York that the Arkansas insurance commissioner had closed the door on Baldwin United. All annuity assets were frozen.

After nearly coming to blows with an unnaturally calm concierge who felt it was his calling to de-stress uptight New Yorkers, I finally got through by phone to my office and booked a flight home. (Remember this was the era before cell phones.) I did not intend to be part of a headline about Paine Webber "Big Shots on the Beach" while our clients might be losing their life savings. On the flight home, I started strategizing. The goal was to assess the potential loss, formulate our response, and calm brokers and policyholders across the country. No small task, but it had to be done.

Back in the office, I began working with my staff and the branches to set up town hall meetings, one region at a time. We brought together groups of clients, sometimes as many as 500 in one room. The insurance regulators devised a plan that would allow us to return the annuity assets at a 3.5% substantially lower interest rate and they had to wait 3½ years to get their money. We held the meetings, listened to the venting of fear and anger, but the minute they heard they were going to get their money back, the anger and fear subsided. And with each encounter, I grew another inch of steel in my backbone. We were not on Wall Street anymore. We were among a sea of faces of real people who were putting their faith in Wall Street. Their candor reminded me of a Mark Twain quote, "Don't tell me about the return on my money—tell me about the return *of* it!" Thankfully, we were able to do just that: tell people that their money would be returned, with interest.

I learned an important lesson, that when people buy a guaranteed product, security is the most important thing to them. Unlike the savings and loan fiasco that would follow in a few short years, or the bailout of 2008, the life insurance industry to its credit was able to absorb the cost of repaying investors in the wake of this disaster.

As part of a reorganization of Paine Webber following Baldwin United, I reported to the new sheriff in town, Bob Benmosche. Bob was hired to lead Paine Webber's competitive efforts to match Merrill Lynch's nascent Cash Management Account (CMA). The CMA was a game-changing vehicle that brought together brokerage and banking in a new way, providing an incentive for clients to consolidate their assets with a single firm. Despite skepticism in the brokerage community, CMA proved to be the "killer app" of financial services in the 1980s.

After the "re-org," at first I was concerned that I would lose my job despite the positive resolution I had helped devise for our annuity clients. But Bob was an observant and shrewd business man. He noticed the due diligence books on my desk. He asked me what I saw there. When I told him that one of our annuity carriers had some issues that made me uncomfortable, he reviewed the material for himself.

"We will stop sales from this company immediately," he concluded.

I agreed with his conclusion, but I felt duty bound to explain to him that the head of the company in question was a tour de force on Wall Street, and he was a personal friend of our own company's president. I will always remember the events that followed.

We called this titan of Wall Street in for a meeting. As he stepped from the elevator, his very presence was intimidating. I felt every inch the junior executive. I knew that we had called him there to end our relationship. Of course, in hindsight, I realize he was nobody's fool; he knew it, too. But the ballet continued. Bob strode over and gave him a firm handshake. I felt the bones rematerialize in my wobbly legs. We went to Bob's office and showed our supplier the due diligence. He gave his most accomplished reassurances, but Bob was unmoved. His delivery was polite, professional and firm. We would no longer sell these products. The meeting ended coolly, but cordially, and I escorted him back to the elevators.

Before I could get back to my desk, my office phone was ringing. It was Don Nicholson, our president.

"Joe, I have a friend of mine here. Is it true that we have to stop sales completely?" He asked pointedly. I asked his indulgence for a moment, and I went to buttonhole Benmosche.

"Tell him we'll be right up. And, bring that report." Bob ordered. He was clearly peeved by this tactic.

We arrived in the executive suites (Oz, we called it) and were announced. Nicholson rose behind his desk and motioned to the chairs opposite him. As we were sitting, Bob began, "This young man found trouble here. We can't sell these products. Sales need to stop immediately, right, Joe?"

With such a forceful ally I could only speak with integrity, "That's what the due diligence tells me." I said sheepishly.

"So unless you want to run the [expletive deleted] insurance department, we're going to do as he says."

"All right then." Nicholson answered.

Bob Benmosche had taught me to stick to my guns. But, perhaps more importantly, he had been a role model for mentoring young people and for teamwork. After all, I know that Bob had been hired in part to help us to keep our noses clean. He could have taken credit for the discovery. He did not need me in any of those meetings, strictly speaking. But he saw the value in presenting a united front, and he wasn't afraid to acknowledge another person's contribution.

DAWN OF THE INFORMATION AGE

A colleague of mine, Mike Farrell, made a very astute observation about the connection between technology and financial services. He pointed to the 1980s—when the PC was introduced—as the watershed time for data-driven mindset in finance. Virtually overnight conceptual discussions about policy benefits were replaced by illustrations and spreadsheets. Adding the financial catalyst for the perfect storm, interest rates were hovering around fourteen percent, putting more pressure on product development to revisit traditional insurance and investment products. By the 1990s, people were bombarded with choices, not only in finance, but virtually everywhere at every level. Annuities and universal life products with a whole host of fixed and variable rate structures flowed into the mix with equities, options, bonds, and REITs. Now people had to choose how to "allocate investments" even if it was only through an employer's retirement plan. No wonder people were craving information. The average person was ill-equipped to make any of the choices intelligently because they lacked the expertise to guide them. So it is no wonder that just when people were feeling the overwhelming need for information to help them make all these choices, personal computer technology found such a receptive audience.

The 80s and 90s put computers in the spotlight in offices and homes across America. Spreadsheets that had once only churned out of huge backroom operations now danced on desktop screens in kitchens and cubicles alike. It gave us immediate access to information—the information revolution we had been waiting for. Like most people, I wanted to believe that if people just had the right information, they would make the right choices.

24

But, I could see the double-edged sword of an increasing focus on statistics and charts—"clinical" data. All the attention was on performance and numbers.

Just a few years earlier I had turned to MetLife to explore the possibilities of applying my experience in the brokerage environment to an insurance company. MetLife was appealing because it was a company I had come to respect for the reliability of its product offerings, and because I felt the need to come home to the insurance business. Once again, I had followed my personal need for security into a company where I felt that the security of the clients was a top priority.

When has a choice for personal fulfillment or security in your own life been tied to the security of others?

This brings us full circle to my dilemma that autumn morning in 1998. I had helped institute financial planning at MetLife, and it was succeeding to a point. But I still felt something was missing from the sales equation in our financial planning process. More "information" was just reinforcing the mistaken impression that what mattered were numbers. I hadn't yet realized how to express it, but somehow I knew it had to be about the people, about the stories, the lives and legacies and generations that are affected by those numbers on a page. We were focusing on communication when what we needed was connection. Somehow the clues were hidden in the faces of those relieved annuity clients whose faith in a sound investment had been validated. There were clues in the missteps of Baldwin United and within my own story.

But at that moment, I was looking at charts and graphs and wrestling with the message that our reps were taking out into the field. Now that people had all this information at their fingertips, did they really have what they needed to make sound financial choices? Was the information giving them an advantage or paralyzing them with data?

In the midst of my questioning, a memory from the early 90s came flooding back to me. It was a personal encounter I had, one that changed my attitude about questioning my own personal choices in life. Until this moment, I had thought of it as part of my own personal journey. I had not seen the potential relevance to the professional conundrum I was considering.

II.

Are You My Mother?

*Computers [sic and their data] are like Old Testament gods;
lots of rules and no mercy.*

—Joseph Campbell

*He is a poor son whose sonship does not make him desire
to serve all men's mothers.*

—Harry Emerson Fosdick

Harry Fosdick, a key figure in an early twentieth century movement called the Social Gospel, understood that a parent's great joy is found in a child who serves the greater good. My career, especially my years at MetLife, have allowed me to do just that. And I came to realize that I hoped this would make me a better son in the eyes of my own mother.

From as far back as I can remember, I looked up to my mother. She was the person I most admired and whose admiration meant the most to me. In these past few years, I have come to realize much more about my relationship with my mother and how I came to believe that the things I do for others—particularly those who need an advocate—are the things that would make my mother most proud of me.

As we consider the patterns in our lives, Joseph Campbell provides some interesting food for thought. In his masterwork, "The Hero's Journey," Campbell points out similar themes and patterns that are shared among all the great folklore and myths from around the world. Across the widest possible range of cultures, stories tell of a hero who passes through milestones that are remarkably similar in their sequence and significance. Campbell was clear that the earliest moments in a person's life begin the shaping process that will ultimately reveal interconnected patterns among the seeming randomness of our lives. Our earliest influences—parents, siblings, teachers, guides—contribute to our conscious and subconscious choices. I had no stronger influence than my mother.

All heroes, it seems, undergo a transformative encounter with a wise mentor—think Yoda in *Star Wars*—who gives the hero a "sacred gift" that imbues him with a power he had not previously known. The memory that came back to me that morning in '98, I might call my Yoda moment.

> One night I was visiting my alma mater Fordham University when I spotted an old friend and former teacher of mine. Although I didn't realize it at the time, this was a particularly important meeting for me—and it definitely was not one I had on my calendar. As we caught up on mutual acquaintances, and discussed the unseasonably nice weather, my friend asked me what I was up to professionally. I told him that I had recently started working at MetLife. He asked me if I enjoyed my work. I was happy that I could tell him that I did. Then he asked if I ever wondered whether I had made the right choice in my career. At the time, the question caught me up short. I'm not really an introspective guy, I thought.
>
> "Why?" I asked.
>
> His answer surprised me. "Not a day goes by when I don't consider my choices and challenge myself about my vocation." He said flatly. "I ask myself tough questions because I have taken on a big responsibility in this life. I feel that I owe it to the people who count on me."
>
> In that moment, my old friend opened a door for me. I didn't walk through it right away, but I saw the little crack of light ahead of me. He was saying that questioning and challenging yourself is healthy and necessary, and it has the potential to make you better at what you do. It may even help you understand why you do what you do.

What questions do you have about your career path? Do you sense any tension between who you are and what you do?

At the time, I had to smile. "But Father," I chuckled, "You're 87 years old. Don't you think you ought to have it down by now?"

"Ah," he replied, looking over his spectacles and right into my soul, "You don't remember the quote I used in class? 'A life unexamined isn't worth living.'"

The memories of my days in his college classroom came flooding back. You see, this friend who had once been my instructor at Fordham was also a Jesuit priest, who had spent his life serving God and others. Now he was here at this crossroads in my journey reminding me that Socrates himself tells us self-examination makes life worth living.

Obviously, not everyone follows the same path in life. We aren't all priests, and we aren't all outliers. But we can all take valuable lessons from the journeys of others. Father Rushmore affirmed for me the importance of questioning for questioning sake—and I didn't even realize I was looking for that affirmation. From there, I began to notice the voices of many others who saw the benefit of questioning. So I embraced it. I read and watched and listened to the questions.

I began to see that I was doing something with my life that I could feel good about. Joseph Campbell would call it, "Following your bliss." But I hadn't made the connection yet between the personal and the professional implications of all I was learning. So, from a business perspective, I still did not know why it was right. I still could not reconcile everything I saw going on around me with my personal sense of well-being. But I had turned a corner and begun a new phase of my life in which the questions became my allies.

One big question had been answered. And a lifetime of fruitful questioning had begun.

Before I had even made the connection between Father Rushmore's counsel and the situation at hand for the MetLife financial planning practice, I had already begun to apply the same hungry curiosity to exploring expert perspectives on related topics in the financial industry. In the next few pages, I'll be introducing some of those who influenced my thought process and helped me evaluate priorities for financial planning. Nick Murray, a prominent financial author, gave us much valuable information about behavioral economics. It was Murray who opened my eyes to what had troubled me with data-based sales theories. When he came to present without a single graph or chart, focusing instead on investor behavior and the emotions that motivate people, it was as though I heard the first tumbler click into place, unlocking a new way to connect with clients. Nick Murray's emphasis on behavioral economics focuses on the premise that people make bad financial decisions based on emotional reactions like euphoria and panic. Murray suggests that a paradigm of "selection and timing" has put both financial professionals and clients into a performance derby that is impossible to achieve, simply because it is not a goal. He states that financial professionals should focus on managing client behavior rather than performance.

STORIES THAT INFLUENCE

Each of the stories in this section tie back to the underlying point that you can make a difference in someone else's life. A long time agent and financial planner named Jack Dempsey shared a story of a young woman who definitely did her financial planning from the heart.

With Love, from China

My client—we'll call her Sally—contacted my office to discuss insurance for her small business, a Christmas tree farm. I invited her in to my office to meet face to face. As we talked about the right policy for her business, I asked her about her retirement plan. She had none. "Well, your employer really ought to provide a retirement plan," I joked. In all seriousness I explained that at her young age (30 years old) retirement savings would accumulate over her lifetime, and that as a self-employed person, she would have to consider things that another employer would otherwise do for her. After she set money aside for retirement, Sally also agreed and chose a $100,000 universal life plan with her mother as the beneficiary. Sally told me that she wanted to be sure her Mom was taken care of if anything happened to her because her Dad hadn't done that. When he died at a young age, her mom had been thrown back into the work force as a school cook to support herself and her two young daughters.

Sally was still in her early thirties when she called me again to say that she had found herself in a position to purchase her aunt's Christmas decoration shop as a complement to her successful tree farm. She had entered an installment plan with her aunt for a purchase price of $160,000. She wanted to be sure that it was paid if for any reason she was unable to make the payments. So, we covered the business with annual convertible term. I delivered the policy that Wednesday.

On that Saturday, Sally was killed in a car crash. Her mother received the $100,000, which she placed in an annuity that allowed her to retire and draw a comfortable income. I delivered the $160,000 to Sally's aunt, who was in poor health and able to cover her care with the proceeds.

But the story doesn't end there. Due to her aunt's poor health, Sally's sister Diane inherited the business. A few years later I was reviewing the business insurance with Diane when she shared with me another chapter in Sally's story. Because of Sally's careful planning, Diane had inherited the business debt-free. She and her husband had never been able to have children, nor had they had the financial resources to pay for costly fertility or adoption alternatives. But with the business free and clear—and successfully up and running due to Sally—Diane and her husband were able to afford the expense of adopting a beautiful little girl from China. They named her Sally.

As I listened to Diane that day, I realized that the "insurance proceeds" that I had delivered on her behalf were really love letters. The letter to her mother said, "I want to make sure you can retire, Mom. You deserve it and I want to give that gift to you." The letter to her aunt said, "I know you can't afford to have me drop the ball with these payments. You've worked hard for your business. I honor that commitment and I want to make sure that I live up to my word." And the love letter to Diane said, "I trust you with the businesses that were such a huge part of my life, but I don't want to saddle you with a financial burden that will just make things harder." But the letter that Sally didn't even know she was writing was to her niece and namesake. That letter said, "Welcome to the family. You will never know me, but I live on through you."

Csaba Sziklai is a psychologist and the founder of the Advocacy System who explored self-esteem issues among his clients, many of whom came from the insurance industry. Sziklai stresses the importance of positive reinforcement and relationship-building in client interactions, again connecting to the humanity of the interaction, not the transaction that it triggers. Sziklai's core message is built around the importance of being an advocate, especially for those who may not normally have a voice in a financial decision, but who will be deeply affected by its outcome: the spouses, children, and families (or business partners).

Sziklai was the other revelation about being in the insurance business. He made the observation that many insurance professionals were not being honest about what they did for a career. Some were even embarrassed about being in the insurance business and, as a result, came off insincere to clients and themselves.

We experience many clients who are in denial of their own mortality. Sziklai's Advocacy System builds scripts that reinforce that the work an insurance professional does is something to be proud of, not ashamed.

In this story from a *Financial Advisor,* T.J. Rogers highlights the importance of advocacy in the way that Sziklai describes it.

Getting Priorities Straight

On September 10, 2001, my wife and I were spending a romantic week in Paris before returning to get our children back to school the following week. That night, we were having a beautiful dinner, black tie, sitting in a beautiful restaurant. The next day was September 11—the September 11—and back at home in New York all hell had broken loose. Travel restrictions kept us in France for another five days before we could get home.

Being separated from the children was the hardest part for us. They were eight and nine at the time. The next morning when phone service was restored, we called them. My daughter got on the phone and said that the father of her best buddy from school was on one of the airplanes that hit the buildings. Although I didn't know him well, this was a person I had seen almost every day dropping off his kids or picking them up. Like so many New Yorkers, I had that "there but for the grace of God" feeling. What a nightmare.

A couple of days after we got home, we had the little girl over for a sleepover with our daughter. We invited her mom over for breakfast the next morning. While we were all sitting around the breakfast table, I offered my help with any issues dealing with her husband's death. I explained that I was in the insurance business and I assured her that I would be happy to help her with any claims issues or whatever she needed. At that point she opened up and told us about his situation, and what he had for life insurance—which was apparently, not much. She said she had to think about what she was going to do next and what kind of job she was going to get and whether or not she had to sell the house. The house needed work.

As she was talking, in my mind's eye I was picturing her late husband in the schoolyard. This was a guy that I would look at and say, 'He would be a nice guy to have as a client.' But it was one of those situations where it's easy to talk yourself out of starting the conversation. You think to yourself, 'I don't want to approach somebody in the school yard. He is the father of my daughter's friend. The timing isn't right.' Well, obviously I didn't approach him. And now I was wondering, "What if…." If I had talked to him about his planning, and he was obviously inadequately covered, maybe he would have purchased some insurance from me. If he'd spent $50 a month on a million of term, his wife's life and his daughter's life would now be dramatically changed for the better. The moral of that story is: Don't be afraid to tell that person about what you do. Don't ever put yourself in a situation where something like this happens and you regret not making that phone call.

I didn't cross that schoolyard. Maybe I was afraid of the rejection. I put my pride first. Now, when I see these kids trooping into school, I put them first. The parents of my children's friends are always on the list of people I talk to about life insurance and financial planning. It isn't a difficult conversation now that I lived through the story of this little girl and her mom. I just picture the little girl and my commitment swallows up my pride.

Daniel Pink, with his ground-breaking look at the relevance of right-brain (emotional) and left-brain (analytical) thought, allowed me to put my own perspective into the context of our evolving culture. I came to believe that my lifelong discomfort with performance-based investing and investing by the numbers, if you will, tied in precisely with the emerging opinions of the day. Intuition, the purview of the stepchild "right brain," is demanding equal attention as we refine our approach to providing financial services. Dan Ariely, an economist who has asserted the importance of emotion, specifically as it applies to economic theory, declared "The End of Rational Economics" in his article of the same name in the Harvard Business Review. I agree with Daniel Pink when he suggests that we need a "Whole New Mind" as we move into the heart of the 21st century where intellect may actually take a back seat to intuition.

Here were experts (these are just a few key examples) from different fields—psychology, economics, and sociology—with a common thread that became increasingly obvious to me: intuition and emotion are central to all human decisions and interactions.

My focus in the financial arena has always been to help find ways to protect individuals for the long term. Taking the long view with people comes naturally when you have a relationship with them.

Insurance products are designed to take care of human needs. I like to say that the insurance business humanizes the capital markets by paying people money when they need it most. The left brain calculates the odds of dying young and discounts the need for life insurance. The decision to buy life insurance should not be by the math, but by the consequences of the decision. What are the consequences if you die young, get sick, or outlive your money?

First, you have to insure what can go wrong to gain the luxury to invest for what can go right. These decisions are not the domain of the analytical mind, but of the emotional, behavioral mind. Therefore, it was not difficult for me to embrace the wisdom of tapping into intuitive urges as part of a strategy for financial planning.

A Father's Story

A story from MetLife financial advisor Ann Marie Miller illustrates the kind of connection to a deep, intuitive wisdom on both the part of the financial advisor and her client. Ann Marie tapped into the gift of a father to a son to open up a conversation that neither client nor advisor could have known would become so significant.

A father's love for his son, a son's love for his mother, and the woman who shed a light on the significance of

34

both—this is the story of Ann Marie Miller. Ann Marie got a call one day from a client who wanted to cancel a policy. It was understandable. It was a baby policy on this young man who was now in his early twenties. Ann Marie told the young man that she would like to meet him and discuss the cancellation.

"This policy was a gift to you from your father," she reminded him.

A simple reminder that his father had valued his son's life set the stage for a conversation in which the young man realized how life insurance can make a difference. He bought a policy from Ann Marie that day, even though he was a young man, and unmarried. He did it to take care of his mother who had only Social Security to rely on.

When he married, Ann Marie helped him insure his wife, and as their children were born, she wrote policies for each of them. She made sure her client had sufficient coverage as his income and responsibilities increased.

Then one day, the young man's wife called to tell Ann Marie that he had died. She cannot tell this part of the story without tears in her eyes. She left the conference she was attending and flew back to be with the family. As she was sitting around their kitchen table, the emotion was overwhelming. The young man's mother kept repeating in Italian, "My son, my son."

Ann Marie recalls, "To my surprise, all they kept saying was, 'What would we be doing now without you?' And I thought, 'I had no idea that what I had done was so significant.'"

The legacy of a father's love, translated by this caring woman and her wise young client, became the saving grace for a new generation and solace for a mother's loss.

Notice that Ann Marie said she did not realize how significant her actions were. This is the part of the business that needs more emphasis and exposure. If you have not experienced something that Ann Marie had, borrow her experience.

As I continued my research into new insights from outside sources that might help me continue to enhance MetLife's approach, I was soon prompted to revisit the events in my own personal life that might hold hidden insights I could share as well. My intuition told me that some of the answers to my professional questions might come from my personal history.

RUMBLINGS OF THINGS TO COME

Meanwhile, a new century was on the horizon. It seems ironic, from where we sit now, given all that happened in the first decade of the new millennium, but the huge concern at that time was Y2K. Programmers everywhere were fixated on the possibility that databases would be erased wholesale when the internal settings displayed double zeroes in the year fields. Since their inception, computers had been programmed using a two-digit system for month, day, *and* year (MM/DD/YY instead of MM/DD/YYYY). As the year 2000 approached, programmers were in a frenzy to prevent the catastrophe that might occur when the zeroes rolled over like lemons on a cosmic slot machine. Would programs erase themselves on a cue that this was the year "00," signaling a start-over mode? It was no joke. Financial systems, government systems, medical systems, everything faced the same exposure. But 2000 arrived, and the crisis passed.

The press, and particularly the financial press, loves to highlight the crisis de jour, which feeds the aberrant behavior that many investors manifest (euphoria at the top and panic at the bottom). This would be reaffirmed during the tech and subprime mortgage bubbles, which we experienced in the first decade of the century.

Although very few escaped unscathed in 2008 and 2009, at MetLife we were insulated from both the tech markets and the subprime mortgages. And in the late 90s, my attention had been on that crucial question of how to fully realize the vision of financial planning. Interestingly, those questions seemed to have led to the very solutions that helped our clients weather the financial storm of those years.

Yes, I still had my questions in 1999. And thanks to my refreshed memory of Father Rushmore and his wisdom about intellectual curiosity, I was reveling in questions instead of pushing them aside. Then one afternoon, with the new millennium just over the horizon, I found myself on the road in a hotel room down in Florida. I had just checked into my room a few hours before my meeting was scheduled to start. I turned on the TV, and saw a commercial, a public service announcement (PSA) actually:

An elderly woman sits looking out through a lace-curtained window. As the camera pans back, there is a bustle of movers emptying the room. Then, a younger woman escorts the elderly woman to a car. She doesn't say a word, but a voice-over reveals her thoughts. "I know you don't really want me to move in with you. After all I'm his mother, not yours." The younger woman, now in the driver's seat, smiles warmly into the rearview mirror, and the tension dissolves as it becomes clear that the daughter-in-law cares for her mother-in-law and the older woman's fears are unfounded.

As I stared at the screen, in my mind's eye, I saw my wife and my mother playing out a scene from fifteen years earlier. I sank onto the bed and absorbed what I was seeing. I realized that I had never considered how my mother felt about moving in with us. At least, I hadn't considered how it affected her dignity, or whether she questioned our willingness to have her with us.

In that moment, I began to realize that the line between my personal and my professional choices was an illusion. In the coming years, I would replay that PSA in my mind many times to explore the reaction it had evoked in me. There was a reason that I persisted in the insurance business, and it had as much to do with my sense of what was right and ethical as it did with my professional ambition or even any rational decisions I felt I had made. It had everything to do with my mother.

A LIFE INTERRUPTED

At the age of 40, my mother, a woman who had tea at the White House (my father had been an advisor to President Truman) and enjoyed a life of relative prosperity, found herself widowed with four small children. The youngest—myself—was just nine months old. It was 1952, and single mothers were certainly not the norm. But the worst blow, after losing my father, may have come on the day my mother learned that he had cashed in his life insurance policy just a few days before his death. A widow with four children, my mother had no financial cushion. She would have to work.

Without missing a beat, my mother put on a pair of crisp, white gloves and her best hat, and landed a job as a secretary for the local bartenders' union. She worked forty hours a week and kept us in clothes and food, and in our home in the Bronx. She was known as the Duchess of the neighborhood in the decades to come for her regal bearing and her impeccable sense of style. My mother was a trailblazer. She rose to the occasion that fate had handed her, and never let on to us that there was any other way to live.

Years later on that night in Florida, I began to look again at my path through life. I remembered how proud I was of my mother and the way she took care of us. Of course, as a child, I didn't realize that things could have been different if we'd had a financial safety net. But despite her best efforts, certain parts of the situation became clear. After my father's death, we were clearly the poor relations. We couldn't afford a car to visit my cousins. We'd have to take the train or the bus to spend a holiday or vacation. But they would never stoop to come to us in the Bronx. Perish the thought. That sort of thing registers with a kid. And then there was the fact that our stylish clothes weren't so stylish by the time my mother would allow us to buy something new. I began to realize that we were just a little out of step by the time I was in junior high.

But all I had to know was—if my mother could work that hard, I could, too.

At the age of thirteen I got my first job at the neighborhood dry cleaner, working six days a week for the summer, then weekends during the school year. I contributed what I could, and eventually, I worked my way through college. However, the toughest decision my mother had to make was to tell my two sisters that they could not go to college at the appropriate age despite the fact that one of them received a full scholarship. They had to go to work to make sure the "boys" (I have an older brother) could go to college. How do you like that legacy?

I think I made them proud when I got into Fordham University. I was serious about making the most of college. I was never a big kid physically, but I was determined, and I was strong. I made the football team at Fordham in my freshman year. I played offensive guard. It was a position that called for relentless single-mindedness. I didn't look left or right once a play was called. I headed straight into the guy in front of me in my zone. A lot of those guys were a head taller than I was, but that didn't stop me. I had a job to do. It was very clear. And I did it. I guess I did it pretty well because despite my size, I ended up being named All East in 1972 and 1973, and later in 1994, I was inducted into the Fordham Athletic Hall of Fame.

Later on at Fordham, I also played rugby, a sport that ultimately led me to forge relationships I still have today. (More on rugby in a later chapter.) And then there were the jobs.

In the summer of 1971, one of my neighbors in the construction trade sponsored me to work with the New York Iron Workers. In the union vernacular, he was my rabbi. The pay was great, $7 an hour, so I decided to go for it. This time it wasn't my height that was an issue; it was my paralyzing fear of heights. I had to balance up to 700 feet above the ground and for a few days, I was on top of the World Trade Center. On a steel beam about two feet wide, I spent my summer in complete denial. The first building I worked on was 1095 Avenue of the Americas, today's MetLife headquarters. My office is on the 40th floor of that same building today.

Consider what you may have learned from early jobs or experiences. Keeping track of these early times may give you useful clues to situations throughout your life.

My experience as a steel worker not only taught me what it means to face one's fears, it provided me with a front row seat to an incident that would later help me put my finger on the source of trouble in a whole host of situations. I didn't know it at the time, but that summer job in college would teach me as much in one day as some of my classes could in a semester. One day I was up on the beams—we were up to the 44th floor by then. Cranes lifted the steel up from the street and the crane was supported by multiple one-inch cables, in tent configuration (called a guide derrick, seldom used today). When you're in denial every day about how high off the ground you are, you can also get so used to watching these heavy loads travel up and down like pick-up-sticks in a kid's fist, that you let yourself forget that there are laws of nature at play. No matter how strong the cable, or how skilled the crane operator, you should never lose respect for the laws of nature and basic physics. We would walk right under those loads, forgetting that safety codes said to walk around.

There was a rumor that we were beginning to lift heavier loads, because the bosses wanted to get the job done faster. And one day, I had my back to the crane, and I heard this big "clang!" When I turned around, a one inch cable had cut loose from the rig, and was now swishing across the deck where I was standing on a 24-inch beam. I had to avoid it, because if it hit me, it would cut me in half. And at that moment, we were all concerned. Would the crane hold up? Would the engineer be able to lower the steel, which was now halfway up the building? The crane groaned and began to shake. What would happen if the other cables snapped? We were in mid-town Manhattan. We were at the intersection of 42nd Street and Sixth Avenue. How many people would be killed? We were there transfixed—helpless.

There was nothing we could do to stop the impending disaster. One by one the other cables began to snap and the whole load of steel fell into the street. And by some miracle only one person was killed.

For all my fear of heights, I never lost the freshness of that experience—or its lesson about the boundaries and limitations of human enterprise.

During college I also volunteered for Catholic Big Brothers of America, when I wasn't working as a nightclub bouncer with my football buddies. The irony of a guy with no father serving as a father figure was lost on me at the time. But the irony of getting home at 4 a.m., and then meeting a young boy to be his mentor and role model did register. I did what I could, getting these kids to the pool, to the movies. We had some good times. But I also learned at a very young age what all fathers eventually learn: there comes a time when you are not really the person a teenage boy wants sitting next to him in the movies.

I became a Big Brother on the recommendation of none other than Father Rushmore, the same Jesuit priest who years later reminded me to keep questioning every day. It seemed like a small thing at the time, volunteering some of my time to help boys have a male role model in their lives. I hope I did some good for those kids. But like so many things in life, Big Brothers started out as something I wanted to do for others and became a hugely important catalyst in my own life.

I've been married for over thirty years to my wife, Geraldine. She has been there with me through everything I am telling you about in these pages, as a partner in the best sense of the word. And, if I hadn't volunteered for Big Brothers, I might never have met her. She was working for Catholic Charities when I was a Big Brother. We met, and the rest is history.

That would have been more than enough to come out of Big Brothers, but when college was almost over and the time had come to choose a career path, it was my Big Brother connections who pointed me toward the life insurance business. There was a guy who used to play for the New York Giants who was also involved with Catholic Big Brothers. He met me and he said, "This might be a good career for you." I could not have imagined where this decision would lead. I took his advice partly because I looked up to him as an athlete, partly because of my admiration for his involvement with Big Brothers, and partly because it was a job and I needed one.

The company I joined on his recommendation, Home Life, had a college division that allowed you to sell to your peers. When I went in to talk with them, they got all over me to join and it made me feel good. I was the only rep on campus for Home Life.

Soon after that, I was walking up the front walk of one of my first customers—a relative of mine—for what I thought would be a pretty straightforward conversation about the policy we'd talked about over the phone.

When I rang the doorbell, nothing had prepared me for what was to come. I had plowed through linemen, and defied gravity on a sliver of steel, but I did not expect the body blow my own family members delivered that day.

I could tell he was worked up as we walked into the study of their Westchester home. I remember we were facing each other over an antique desk that probably cost more than that family car we couldn't afford at the time. I couldn't understand what he was going on about. Then, his father strode into the room, grabbed the documents out of my hand, and flung them in my face. "How dare you peddle this garbage to my son!" was his message. He went on to disparage me personally, to question my motives, and to run down the company I worked for. It was a tremendous blow.

I never told my mother what happened. But for days I questioned whether this was the right work for me. I wasn't sure there was any job that was worth that kind of assault on my self-esteem. But I stayed with it. I probably thought I knew why at the time. Now I know that answer still laid buried deep inside my subconscious.

I was right to believe that my determination to stay with my job began with my mother. She was the only parent I ever knew, and I wanted to do the right thing by her. But as the stories of my youth and childhood unfolded in my adult mind on the corner of that hotel bed, watching that commercial evoke the image of my mother before my eyes, there was another specter I would eventually have to acknowledge. One of the strongest influences in my life had the biggest impact through his absence. In every story, my absent father reverberated; he wasn't there, yet he shaped my life story.

My mother at work, my sisters at home postponing college, my own early introduction to work—all of it happened because he wasn't there. I was a father figure to young boys without fathers, when I had none of my own. My father wasn't there to tell me what to say to the young boy whose mind was only on girls. On the football field, among the steel workers, my father could not be there. He was not there when another man's father hurled my paperwork and my dignity at my face. He wasn't there. He couldn't help that. But he could have left a very different legacy.

At this moment two trains of thought converged. First, the questions kept bubbling: What had motivated me? Why did I put myself in these positions? What might I have missed in my mother's eyes on the day she moved in with us? Second, a slow burn started, the flames of which would not erupt for another five years.

Have you faced rejection from someone whose opinion mattered a great deal to you? What effect has rejection had on your self-esteem? your work habits?

III.

Coming to Terms

A man is about as big as the things that make him angry.

—Winston Churchill

Sometimes you'll hear people say, "Don't sweat the small stuff." I think Churchill was making the same point in this quote, but from a stronger perspective. When you are in the midst of feeling angry, you may think it is about something small and insignificant when it is actually rooted in something deeper. If you look for the source of your anger, that is sometimes where you can begin to find what really matters to you. I may have thought that the rudeness of someone hanging up on me made me angry during a sales call. But what really makes me angry is that person hanging up on a chance to do what is right for his family. My anger, it turned out, was about the basic injustice to families left without resources at their times of greatest need.

When I tell you that I had never made the connection between my childhood, growing up without my father (or the lost benefits of that insurance policy he cashed in just days before his death), and my choice to go into insurance, you can absolutely believe it. Until I saw that public service announcement with the elderly woman and her daughter-in-law on the television in that hotel room in 1999—more than ten years after I had lost my mother in 1987, almost fifty years since I lost my dad—in my mind, my life story was just that, a story that had played itself out due to circumstances. My career on the other hand, it seemed to me, was more about my choices, my plans, my drive for success.

I showed that video at a fee-based financial planning meeting. I had used material before to tap into an emotional response from an audience. But this was different, as I was tapping into the planners'

43

emotions, I was also experiencing an emotional connection myself. I began to realize then that my own story, and my mother's story could unlock a deeper understanding of the good that financial planners do. Also, a dear friend and MetLife colleague had died. We were all mourning his passing and remembering what he had meant in our lives, and the lives of so many people he had served over the years. But at that very same moment, as we praised our friend for the way he changed lives for the better with his solid advice and commitment, I realized that emotion was not only a presentation approach, it had a place in inspiring sales reps to see how their products can help people.

Then I let the questions begin again. I realized it would be fruitful to look at my life experience from a new perspective. What did any of those things mean? Choices? Plans? Success? How much is in my control and how much "just happens" and how do I tell the difference? And what difference does it end up making to the rest of the world? It turned out that I cared more than I realized about how my choices affect the rest of the world and those around me. And that had everything to do with my choice of a career. Slowly I came to understand that my personal life and my professional life were intertwined in ways I had never imagined. The seeds that had been planted along the way—my mother's courage and my father's absence, my sports experiences, my career path, and the wisdom of experts in professional and philosophical areas—all of these had begun to germinate.

Throughout the 90s, I had sought out the wisdom of experts from a wide range of disciplines. I read voraciously, and I thanked my mentor for giving me that permission I hadn't known I was seeking—to examine my life's journey.

From the time Father Rushmore encouraged me to keep questioning, I had peeled back the layers of my life in a search for meaning. It was inevitable that the search would someday reach its hidden molten core.

In the spring of 2004 when I spoke before the MDRT gathering, I had begun to see the bits and pieces of my life story as something more cohesive than I had previously thought it to be. But my exercise in personal anthropology was reaching critical mass, and no sooner had I started to work on my presentation than I tapped into a hidden vein of anger that had lain far beneath the surface of my tough, determined, professional persona. The anger I felt was a legitimate response to an ancient hurt. But frankly, it surprised me. I knew that

I had to accept it and move on. But for the moment, it was a part of everything I did and said.

I'm including an excerpt from the end of that presentation here. As you read it, picture me with my fists clenched as I shared my own story—and in a sense heard my own story—for the first time. Imagine how it felt to speak to 8,600 people about the father I never knew. It will sound familiar to you now, since you've read the previous pages, but here you will feel the anger that I got in touch with while sharing it for the first time.

> When I was six months old, my very successful attorney father died without life insurance. My mother then had to go out and work as a secretary to raise all of us. She had to make some very hard decisions. You see those girls? (referring to a slide of my sisters and my mom, which you can see on this page.) None of them went to college at the appropriate time, even though one got a full scholarship, because the girls had to work to make sure that the boys could get through school. How do you like that little sibling dynamic? She worked hard. I graduated and then she got sick. Then after she got sick, she began to see that she would become dependent. As my mother would say it, "I would be inconvenient." So she willed herself to die. That is why she is not here to see her son, on the main platform of the Million Dollar Roundtable.
>
> You know what? I don't think that people deserve to go out like that. I want to know, where was the person of significance, the advocate, who could have taken my father, even pushed him up against a wall and said, "Don't you understand you have to have life insurance? I'm advocating for your wife because if you're gone, life could be miserable." Where was the advocate who advocated for my sisters who were denied a college education at the appropriate time? Where was the advocate even for my father, whose younger son stands in front of you now? The only legacy I can tell you that my father left us was he left us alone.
>
> You have to understand what your sacred trust is. You have to overcome your call reluctance. It has to come from the heart to go out and find people like the elderly woman or my mother because you have to protect them. You have to help people. Ask the question they cannot ask unaided

by you, which is, what would happen if I'm not here to be around to take care of my family?

Finally, you have permission to be confrontational with people because you are dealing with their most precious assets—their children and their legacy. If someone is disrespectful of you or treats you like a used car salesman and says you are a pushy salesman, do you know what you tell them? What I do for a living is I protect the innocent when someone dies prematurely. I provide a worry free retirement that people can't outlive. I protect their assets when they get sick. I provide legacy when they die because I live a life of significance. Thank you.

It came out spontaneously in that 2004 presentation to the MDRT. I was channeling a surge of pure rage. I was angry at my father for leaving his family unprotected.

There it was: The undeniable connective tissue between my personal journey and my chosen profession. Who could possibly be better suited to work passionately on behalf of the beneficiaries of insurance clients—as I had done for over three decades—than a person who knew first hand what it meant when those insurance policies weren't in place. It had taken me all these years to fully appreciate how my father's untimely death and unwise decision had set the course of my mother's life—including her ultimate need to have us take her in at the end of her life—as well as the lives of my siblings, and my own. How could I have been unaware of this burr in my saddle, prodding me on to make sure people understand how important it is to remember the ones who are relying on them.

In those moments, like the one my father experienced, when something else seems more compelling, I have always known in the fiber of my being that nothing is more important than insuring the well-being of those who depend on you. That is the basis of our calling in the insurance business: we talk to people about things that are important, not just popular, and about the people who depend on them. We remind them that they cannot know when they won't be there anymore.

FINDING JULIUS

The story of Art Steinberg and his family shows how the reverse situation from my own has had just such an impact for generations. Ira Horowitz was the life insurance agent who sold the policy in this story. Sixty years and three generations later, the family still remembers his name. I don't know if he was aware of the impact he made on this family. I hope he was.

On the night of my brother's bar mitzvah, family members were in from all over to help us celebrate his passage to manhood. It was the summer of 1954. My father was 45 years old—a young man. But that night, he died. It was sudden, unexpected, and it transformed a joyous family gathering into an occasion for mourning.

My mother, like most women at the time, did not work outside the home. Now she had two boys, aged nine and thirteen, a mortgage, and a lifetime of expenses ahead of her. But, my father had met an insurance agent just a few weeks earlier. He had purchased a sizeable life insurance policy for the time. That policy paid a lump sum of $20,000, which more than covered the mortgage; and a continuing monthly benefit of $263 per month.

I know that exact amount because ten years later, in my sophomore year of college, my mother died. But the checks kept coming right through my last month of college. I remember receiving the letter saying that the enclosed payment was the final one. Incredible. I thought how smart my father was to have come up with a plan like that—two sons through college, his wife able to keep them in her own home for the rest of her life.

As I thought about it, although I didn't want to take anything away from my father for making such a good decision, I knew that he was not really educated in financial matters. I realized that the credit was due in large part to that insurance agent, the one who sat him down and said, "You know, Julius, if all of a sudden you're not here tomorrow, what is going to keep your family in their own home and get your boys through college?" My father must have given him the basic numbers to work with, and the result was that it was all paid—right through my graduation. The impact of that is enormous. It goes far beyond the financial aspects of our life. Had my father not done that, my brother and I would not have gotten college educations. I wouldn't have met the woman I married, had my own children—you know, everything is related. So that decision not only affected one generation, it continues through generations. Now all my children have been educated, and I have grandchildren, and they're the beneficiaries, too.

That one agent, 56 years ago, had a conversation that has transformed the lives of multiple generations. As an insurance agent myself, I never lose sight of the potential we have in this business to change lives. My challenge to everyone in this business, especially new agents, is this: find Julius. All of us have an obligation to go out and find our Julius—that person who cares for his or her family, who would never want to leave them unprotected, but who needs you to make it clear how vitally important, how life-changing the choice to purchase insurance can be.

I like to joke around about, "Joe's Interesting and Amazing Facts," my proprietary research that shows, "Guess what? Everybody dies." But the joke is really a way of relieving the tension of an undeniable reality. I don't want to dwell on it anymore than the next person, but we will all die one day. We don't want to sit around and worry about it, but we have to accept it—and prepare for it—because denying it won't change it. My father lost sight of this reality. Maybe the most infuriating part of the story is that he had the policy. There was a time when he grasped the importance of insurance. Then he let it go. And the wheels were set in motion for five lives to change when one ended.

As the roots of my personal anger became exposed, I became furious, in turn, at the lack of recognition for our industry's contribution to the lives of so many people. It was as though my awareness of my personal circumstance as an unprotected child gave me newfound permission and passion to speak on behalf of those children. It resonated in the core of my being. And, my recognition of my mother and my wife in the on-screen scenario of end of life decisions, emboldened me on behalf of those who might benefit from long term care protection.

For years, many insurance professionals have approached prospecting with all the relish of going for a root canal. They do all but apologize for engaging in a conversation that every responsible adult ought to have. Somewhere along the line, many in our profession bought into a skewed point of view about the work we do. In the heat of my anger, I had a flash of clarity: We shouldn't feel like beggars—we should feel more like saints.As Csaba Sziklai would say, we are "advocates who have little or no voice in the decision to buy insurance despite the fact that their lives can be seriously affected by their presence or absence thereof." As I watched the reaction of the audience to that 2004 presentation, I felt that I had been as surprised and moved by the passion I was expressing as anyone in the room.

As part of the Living a Life of Significance program at MetLife, along with The American College, we asked agents to tell us the stories they considered pivotal in their careers. One of those stories, submitted to us by Bob Weaver, a 60-year veteran of the business, makes the case for self-esteem in our industry very powerfully. I will share it with you here:

In the Service of Others

Back in 1945, two young Air Force pilots were hitchhiking back to base after a leave. It was the dead of winter in central Massachusetts, and the snow was drifted well over their heads on the side of the road. The two had just completed rigorous training and had qualified for a prestigious unit, ready for deployment. A good Samaritan pulled over and let them into his car. The kindly driver told the pair that he would need to make a few stops along the way, but he would gladly take the young men to Springfield if they would have a patience for his schedule.

After the second stop, the driver explained that he was collecting life insurance premiums from his clients (these were just a few dollars a piece back then) and he preferred to do it in person so he could stay in touch with each person he served. Before thinking much about it, one of the soldiers responded as he might have to one of the guys in the barracks—without much respect, but intending no real harm.

"That's quite a racket you've got there," he quipped.

The driver's face changed abruptly, and he steered the car off the road, so close to the snow bank that the passenger door would not have opened.

"You can climb out over me, or you can stay here and listen," he said sternly. "The next stop I'm going to make, I won't be collecting a payment; I'll be delivering one. Even though it won't bring back the husband and father of that household, it will be more money than they've probably ever seen in one check. And it will make all the difference in the lives of that family. So, make no mistake, what I do is no racket. I am serving my clients in a way that can

49

keep them going when they need it most. You boys should understand the importance of service. Am I right?"

They did understand. And one of those Air Force pilots went on to become an extremely successful producer, who considered this story the one that changed his life and allowed him to find a career that gave his life significance for more than sixty years after that night. That young pilot was Bob Weaver.

In the story, I can hear the same passion of the agent who inspired another man to devote sixty years to following those footsteps. I realized then that I had to press myself to understand more about what I was experiencing so that I could articulate it in a way that would benefit more people.

The Steinberg family has another story that underscores the value of facing painful moments with courage. While I truly appreciated Art Steinberg's first story, when we taped him, he seemed distracted. I had no idea at the time that his son, Justin, had recently died. So the legacy of Ira Horowitz continues. This is Justin's story.

Justin's Story

Every scholarship represents a person or group who wanted another person to have the chance at pursuing their dreams. You may have walked past a plaque or read a graduation program and wondered about an unfamiliar name. This is the story behind one of those names. Justin Steinberg, in the words of his father, was "just the greatest son. I really can't remember him ever giving us a bad time. And his personality…he just had the best sense of humor. He was fun to be around."

Justin was never able to graduate from college. Six weeks before the end of his sophomore year, just before finals, he fell into the final relapse of a long, debilitating, and ultimately fatal illness. Throughout his ordeal, Justin always thought of others first. He worried that he might trouble the nurses. He was concerned about his parents. But they were able to reassure him, and it truly gave him great comfort to know, that the financial hardship was alleviated by a policy his parents had bought for him as a child—one with a disability waiver that paid the premium while he was ill and guaranteed his legacy to others.

As Justin's parents faced the inevitable loss of their son, his mother made a "nonnegotiable, irreversible decision" to honor her son's memory in a way that reflected his selfless, giving nature. Knowing how Justin loved learning, and specifically Mary Washington College (now University of Mary Washington), his mother determined that they would establish the Justin Steinberg scholarship there. Funded by the proceeds of his life insurance policy and nurtured for posterity by continued investment, the scholarship fund in Justin's name provides a needs-based award that will enable one student each year to attend the historic, private University just a few hours south of our nation's capitol and gain an excellent higher education that they might not otherwise have.

The first recipient, one of ten children in a Navy family, wrote the Steinberg's a beautiful letter of appreciation. They knew they had made the right decision.

Justin's name will live on for generations. "Long after we're gone, students will still receive the Justin Steinberg scholarship," His mother says proudly. More than his name, Justin's generous spirit lives on and branches out into the lives of each student and their families and accomplishments and contributions to society.

"That is the miracle of life insurance," Justin's father states plainly. "The scholarship is really a way for Justin to live on because it is just the way he was. He cared about people."

In our Western culture, with our emphasis on individualism, we focus on our separateness from other people and from nature. In the Native American traditions, the interconnectedness of all living things is seen to bring harmony in one's life. This viewpoint sustained the Native American people through many trials. In time, I would come to value the words of the native American leader, Chief Seattle, as the quintessential example of coming to terms with a painful experience. Chief Seattle, for whom the city of Seattle, Washington, is named, was a brave and eloquent leader of the Suquamish and Duwamish tribes who controlled much of the area around the northern Puget Sound during the 1800s. He was greatly respected by his own people, and his prophetic vision of a world without respect for nature and the environment have earned him lasting respect far beyond the cultural boundaries of his time. The words of his legendary speech delivered in 1891 have inspired historians and environmentalists for more than a century. I've included the version offered as a modern interpretation of the speech by Ted Perry here:

> We just got word from your President back in Washington that he wants to buy our land. But how can you buy and sell the sky? The land? The idea is strange to us. All parts of this earth are sacred to my people. Every shining pine needle. Every sandy shore. Every mist in the dark woods. Every meadow are all holy in the memory and experience of my people. We are part of the earth, and it is part of us. The perfumed flowers. These are our sisters. The bear, the deer, the eagle, these are our brothers. Each ghostly reflection in the clear waters of the lake tells of the events and memories in the life of my people. The waters murmur with the voice of my grandfather's father. The rivers, these are our brothers. They carry our canoes and feed our children. If you buy our land, know that the air is precious to us. Know that the air shares its spirit with all the life it supports. The wind that gave my great grandfather his first breath also received his last sigh. This we know.
>
> The earth does not belong to man. Man belongs to the earth. All things are connected like the blood that binds us together. Man did not create the web of life, he simply is a strand in it. What he does to the web, he does to himself. Your destiny is a mystery to us. What will happen when all of the buffalo are slaughtered? What will happen when all of the secret corners of the forest are heavy with the scent of many men? And the view of the ripe hills is blotted by talking wires? It's the end of living, and the beginning of survival. When the last Red Man and his wilderness is gone, and his memory is that of a cloud going over the prairie? Will there be any memory of my people left? We love this land like the newborn loves its mother's heartbeat.
>
> So if you buy our land, love it as we have loved it. Care for it as we have cared for it. Hold in your mind the memories of the land when you receive it, and preserve it for all children. Love the land the way God loves you, because this we know, no man be he Red Man or White Man can stand alone. Because we're brothers after all.

This speech was delivered at a time when this proud man and his people were about to lose everything. (The original transcription by Dr. Henry Smith, uses the "flowery Victorian language of the day," but is considered quite accurate by the native peoples of the region.) Yet his philosophy of balance with nature caused him to pity the civilization that was taking the land. You see in the Western tradition, we view nature as something to be conquered. That's why we cut down the forest and kill the buffalo, and defy gravity by lifting the heavy loads of steel and defy all reason by offering subprime mortgages to people for whom the financial burden would become to great to bear. In a culture without harmony, you can be enriched, but never fulfilled.

Chief Seattle gives the best definition of what the Million Dollar Round Table (MDRT) calls "the complete person": knowledge of where you came from, stewardship while you are here, and legacy when you die. Notice how he gives human attributes to parts of nature. To him, the whole planet was alive. Also know his reference to the web of life. Look at the role Ira Horowitz played in the web of life. He insured Julius Steinberg and his proceeds ensured his son, Art, a good life. Ira's legacy continues when Art insures his son, Justin, who falls ill and unfortunately dies. The proceeds of Justin's policy assures the college tuition of a young woman and many more to come. Ira Horowitz story spans four generations and they all know his name!

Tell me another profession that can have a legacy lasting four generations? The key question is, did Ira Horowitz realizes this? We will never know, but Ira has given you a gift of witnessing the generational impact your actions can have while avoiding what Thomas Carlyle called "the tragedy of life."

The tragedy in life is not what men suffer; it's what they miss.

—Thomas Carlyle

Why would you be in this business and miss this impact?

DIGGING DEEPER

The best way to deal with anything painful is to face it head on, as Chief Seattle did. No sooner had I made this realization than my mind filled with images of my days on the football field. Now, the insurance business has no shortage of sports-related stories and metaphors. I knew that part of my story would fit neatly into one of these formulaic tales. There is no doubt that my head-down determination to take out the guy in front of me, no matter what his size, had been translated into a similar drive and motivation in situations like getting back to New York from that disastrous Paine Webber Club Med trip I mentioned earlier.

But there was more to my memories about college sports than clichés about driving success. When I played football at Fordham, I literally played the exact position that was once filled by the legendary Vince Lombardi. Lombardi died of cancer the year I started college. Before then, he had been a winning coach for the Green Bay Packers. When he died, the Super Bowl trophy was renamed in his honor.

When I was playing in his spot, I like to joke that Lombardi almost came to life for me. You can imagine the influence this larger than life figure had on young men of my age, growing up watching and playing football. So to stand on the field in his position gave me a sense of tremendous responsibility and connection to the Hall of Famer. The tougher the situation, the more I could hear Lombardi in my ear, feel him over my shoulder. When I made All East, I gave a nod to my "patron saint of offense," Vince Lombardi.

But, perhaps the most meaningful lesson I learned from playing college sports came from the fact that I had experience on both the football and the rugby teams. Traditionally American football, while being a team sport, emphasizes the starting team. Vince Lombardi would say "I don't play my eleven best, I play my best eleven." It suggests teamwork. The difference is that in football only the first team plays. Many college and high school football players hardly ever get to play. Further there is no way you meet the other team. After the game you never see them. The culture of American Football is such that meeting others is incidental to playing the game.

In rugby, everybody plays. If you're not on the "A" team, you are on the "B" team or the "C" team. It is customary after the game to party with the other team. You meet and forge relationships with people who have a common interest. So in the rugby culture, playing the game is incidental to meeting and socializing with others.

After playing rugby for 2 years, I had commented on this fact. The player that was most memorable to me was number 57 from Georgetown. We both started as freshman. So once a year for 4 years, we would line up against each other. He was distinctive because he had no teeth in his head except his two canines. It was like lining up against Count Dracula. We would absolutely kill each other. I was reminded of the Ali/Frazier fight.

At the end of the game, we would seek each other out and say see you next year. After senior year, we lost touch. In 1976 we were playing the Harvard Business School. At the end of the game, I put on a Fordham football wind breaker. My opposite number looked at the insignia and asked me if I played for Fordham. I said yes. We looked at each other and he pulled his teeth out—it was him! What a great reunion.

There's an important point to make about the player experience between football and rugby. The cultures are different. One emphasizes the game while the other emphasizes relationships.

One last comment on American football and rugby: Having played both it is my opinion that American football is more violent. The equipment is not protection—it is a weapon. Football is a game of *collision*, predicated on the taking and defending of territory. As a result there are more frequent all out collisions. Play ends, the teams regroup, catch their breath and do it all over again. Rugby is a game of possession. The key is to keep possession of the ball—to keep passing it or to set it up for the forwards to keep possession of the ball. The ebb and flow of yardage is less important. As a result you don't always get the *consistent* big hits. Just look at all the recent revelations about concussions in American Football.

It's a function of culture. A while back, I said that I was probably hired at MetLife based on knowledge and experience with annuities in the investment world. But my main influence has been as much about culture and human behavior as product. When I first arrived at MetLife after years in the fast-moving Wall Street environment, the pace seemed glacial to me. Remembering the importance of connecting with people to foster a common understanding, I wanted to set up conference calls with agents around the country. In 1990, MetLife—like many big companies—didn't have the kind of phones you need for these calls. My response was to send somebody out to Radio Shack to buy one. It seemed like a simple thing, but it was revolutionary at the time. With a $200 conference phone, we broke through layers of hierarchy and years of siloed, separatist behaviors. Agents, actuaries, investment department reps, all on the phone together, talking about what they actually do, instead of fantasizing about who is keeping whom from what they want to do. Before these calls—which became standard practice—everyone had communicated by letter. Now, people were able to value each other's contributions, exchange ideas, and get things done more effectively.

**What barriers have you faced that you might break down
with a bit of creativity?**

We sometimes fail to appreciate how rapidly our culture has changed in the past twenty years. Some of those changes came with advances in technology; some came through other forces. For example, the huge influx of women in the workforce has changed business culture in ways I wish my mother could have experienced. I remember all too well how casually my male colleagues would toss off a phrase like, "Let's bring the girls in to take notes." The person who came in would not be a "girl" at all, but a woman who clearly deserved the respect of being treated as a peer. I would always think of my mother, single-handedly raising her four children, and going into work for men who referred to her as a "girl." It's important to remember these advances, so we can keep them intact. Respect is a critical element in a healthy culture. Respect, for coworkers and customers, is just plain good for business.

This brings us to our current situation in the early 21st century. Now, more than ever, the products offered by insurance companies are of tremendous value to today's consumer. People no longer have the kind of security that old style defined benefit plans offered. In addition, the sheer volume of financial choices can be overwhelming for the average person trying to make those sound decisions. Beyond that, the lessons of history continue to demonstrate that people can tolerate volatility (the price one pays for greater long-term total return of equities); they will do better. The problem is getting people to deal with the emotional extremes of euphoria at the top and panic at the bottom.

Clients need a partner—someone or an entity that can talk to them or take some of the volatility away. The real risk people face is not the risk to principal, but the risk to purchasing power. With a life expectancy of thirty years, for a nonsmoking couple of 65 years of age, $100,000 at age 65, needs to be $230,000 thirty years later. That requires people to have some form of an equity position. But how can you help people stay in equities and handle volatility, which time and time again people fail to do?

For the insurance industry, the crises that began in 2007 introduced a perfect opportunity to reassert the value of protection and income products in the face of financial insecurity. To be sure, the crisis was precipitated by the same sort of unsafe practices that always lead to financial crises. In "This Time Is Different,"[2] no less than eight centuries of "financial folly" are documented, which leads me to the conclusion that we will see yet more bubble-and-burst scenarios for as long as human beings deal with financial matters.

In the past, economists almost universally dismissed emotion as a secondary decision-making factor. Increasingly, experts in many fields—science, sociology, and, yes, even economics—are telling us that few important decisions are made without emotion The protection of one's family in the case of death or disability and the protection against the financial burden imposed by long-term care costs are undeniably emotional issues. It would be virtually impossible to have a completely objective conversation about topics like these in which the importance of the issues truly registered with the person whose family's well-being is at stake. My own childhood and my mother's last years are the quintessential stories of how a fateful decision to forego the security of insurance coverage can shape a lifetime. As insurance professionals, part of our responsibility is to make sure people connect their decisions with the faces of those who will be affected by them. Charts, tables, and graphs should come into play only after the personal, emotional connection is made.

Once I started recognizing connections between my personal and professional paths, suddenly I saw them everywhere: the connection between Catholic Big Brothers and my first job at Home Life; my determination on the football field, and my bold step into the department head position at Paine Webber; my respect for my mother and my rejection of sexist comments about "bringing the girls in"; my dedication to life protection products and my anger toward my father.

---

2. C.M. Reinhart and K. Rogoff (2008).

In 2008—when the financial disaster struck—and the financial firms started to teeter like giant dominoes, threatening to flatten the entire economy if they fell—I made the connection that has served me best. This time my office view is from the 40th floor of 1095 Avenue of the Americas—a floor I once walked when it was open steel beams. From that building, in 1971, you'll remember I heard the horrific snapping of the multiple cables succumbing to forces of the heavy load of steel.

From the same building, this time safely behind walls and windows, in 2008, someone came into our meeting and said AIG is about to claim bankruptcy in 30 minutes. The last company that I would have thought to have trouble was AIG. It had a great track record for profits and earnings. They always seemed to be doing the "right thing." I guess being in that building I instantly thought of the load too heavy. This time it wasn't steel, it was subprime mortgages. Rather than defying gravity, some very smart people decided to defy common sense. They thought they could give mortgages to people they didn't know had the ability to pay the mortgages back. The premise was that real estate prices would continue to rise. Since they could securitize the mortgages, they would sell them to other institutions who should have known better because they wanted higher yield.

For a while, it worked, but the load was too heavy. The first cable to snap was Countrywide, then Bear Stearns, then Lehman Brothers, then Merrill Lynch, and finally AIG. All of those employees were betrayed by senior management's decision to defy human nature.

In the West, nature is something to be conquered. That's why, as Chief Seattle said, we kill the buffalo, or in construction, we lift the heavy load, or in the world of finance, we package financial instruments doomed for failure. In the East, the predominant thought is to be in harmony with nature—to have balance.

The lesson of the crane is simple—it reaffirms one of my basic principles. I call it the Fairness Doctrine. There are three parties to the trade: there's a client, an intermediary, and a company. All three have to be a little sad.

If the client is ecstatic, you are giving it away. If the intermediary is ecstatic, we're paying too much for it; and if the company is ecstatic, you couldn't sell it if you life depended on it. Balance between the three competing problems involved is the art of successful product development.

In that moment I saw in the clearest terms that there is nothing new under the sun. Just as rogue insurance companies such as Executive Life and Baldwin United were invested in junk bonds and affiliated assets, so the wild revenue projections of the internet venture capital market, and the subprime real estate market that was not in the business of selling homes for people to live in, but as though they were so many game pieces on a Monopoly board, similar to the overburdened cables could not hold more weight than it was designed to hold, it all came crashing down.

Financial experts can tell you these things. You can read charts, graphs and tables that demonstrate trends and confirm projections. But I would argue there is nothing more valuable than making that intuitive connection between the information you are digesting and the emotional, real-life connections to your own experience.

How were you or someone you know personally affected by the Great Recession of 2008? What have you learned from this downturn?

For my part, I felt fortunate that I had pursued my fascination with philosophy, spirituality, and other intellectual and thought-provoking topics. I had not realized that these endeavors might become useful for insurance and business professionals beyond my ability to share some relevant quotes in the course of my speaking engagements. My passion for learning was an exercise in personal growth, or so I thought. Now the concepts, ideas and expressions I had become familiar with over the years found a new resonance as the right brain, left brain conversation moved into the mainstream of scientific and psychological circles.

As I write this book, the Gulf of Mexico has suffered a devastating ecological and economic impact from a damaged deep-water well. The full effects will not be known for years to come. I cannot help but be reminded of the sage commentary attributed to Chief Seattle on the dangers of environmental abuses. "Whatever befalls the earth, befalls the sons of the earth." Whether a man-made disaster that affects the ecology of the planet, or a man-made financial crisis that threatens the well-being of a nation, our actions never happen in a vacuum. When the culture of a society or an industry fails to recognize our basic interconnection, damage is done that affects us all.

It is important to take actions that help to restore harmony and respect the laws of integrity as well as nature. One person's—or one company's actions—may not prevent bad things from happening, but they can add to the good side of the equation that keeps things in balance.

IV.

Tapping the Well Within

Be patient toward all that is unsolved in your heart and try to love the questions themselves like locked rooms and like books that are written in a very foreign tongue. Do not now seek the answers, which cannot be given you because you would not be able to live them. And the point is, to live everything. Live the questions now. Perhaps you will find them gradually, without noticing it, and live along some distant day into the answer.

—Rainer Maria Rilke, *Letters to a Young Poet*

We shall not cease from exploration, and the end of all our exploring will be to arrive where we started and know the place for the first time.

—T. S. Eliot

I was fortunate to have Father Rushmore in college to give me permission to question, and later in life to remind me of the benefit of continually questioning. If you don't already have someone in your life that has done the same for you, I hope to do it in this book. The quote here reminds us that we "live the questions." Answers come much later in life, if at all. To be impatient for answers is to miss out on life. But to rush around so much that you forget to question is perhaps the greatest loss.

I want to encourage you to be patient with those questions that bubble up every day. They are like an internal spring, filling a well of insights from which you can draw throughout your life and career. In this chapter, I will use the milestones that mark my personal journey to turn the spotlight on your own journey. You will recognize the stories from earlier chapters, but more importantly my hope is that you also recognize there universal qualities as they apply to you. At the end of the day, this book is not supposed to help you learn more about Joe Jordan—it's supposed to help you learn more about yourself.

The Vietnamese Buddhist monk Thich Nhat Hanh advises those who are angry to embrace their anger rather than push it away. This Eastern wisdom is sometimes difficult for a Western mind to grasp. We Westerners typically categorize emotions into those that are good and those that are bad. This may cost us opportunities to listen to parts of ourselves that have important lessons to teach us.

Once my own anger welled to the surface, I had little choice but to confront it. In doing so I found it had much to teach me. My internal conflict had brought new perspective to my understanding of some seminal moments in my life. In speaking with other insurance professionals over the years, I have heard plenty of anger and frustration, if only in the undercurrents of some conversations. If we are honest with ourselves, we know that we have put ourselves in the line of fire, and we sometimes wonder why. Why do we take the risk of hearing *no* hundreds of times in the course of our careers? Take a few minutes to go back and look again with me at some of the answers I've uncovered, but translate them to your own experience. Answer the questions at the end of each section, and you'll begin to see the outline emerging of your of life of significance.

A MOTHER'S STRUGGLE AND A SON'S VOCATION

One common thread throughout my life has been a determination that has come to my aid in critical moments. I have come to realize that this determination was fueled by my mother's strong example and my deep-seated unwillingness to let circumstances stop me. In this way, I was able to mentor fatherless boys although fatherless myself; to step into the shoes of the great Vince Lombardi; to climb stories high on the frame of a skyscraper, despite a dreaded fear of heights; pick up my broken ego from the floor of my cousin's study and go on to a successful thirty-plus year career in insurance. In a way, both my parents gave me a piece of what I needed to maintain single-minded determination. My father planted a seed of anger that ultimately fueled some good results. But it was my mother's stoic stick-to-itiveness that instinctively kicked in at critical decision points and steered me on toward my better self.

Determination may come naturally or it may require a conscious, concerted effort. In my experience, I have seen both. Make no mistake; it takes determination to work in this business. Determination comes more easily when you are convinced that what you are determined to do is the right thing.

Who and what gave you some of your earliest inspiration?

How you have dealt with anger or unwanted emotions in your life?

What sources of strength do you draw from in your own history?

THE CRANE AND THE CRASH

In my personal story, determination brought me through many circumstances—sometimes with tangential benefits that I could not have anticipated. For example, my determination to earn the money I needed for college put me in a unique position to face my fears. I am still afraid of heights, but fear is not my master. I know that if a situation demanded it, I could pass through fear to achieve the necessary end.

I could not have known that my very presence on those towering girders would put me where I needed to be to observe one of the most profound events of my life when that crane gave way. The echo of that terrible construction accident in 1971 never left my ears or my psyche. As I think of it now, I have come to realize that it taught an invaluable lesson. As a metaphor for what happens when limits are breached, the snap of the cables, and all that led up to it, has become an internal barometer, allowing me to anticipate dangerous trends in markets, in relationships and in life. I may not be able to prevent them from happening, but I can avoid walking under the load on its way up and help others to do the same.

I have talked about the way that the nauseating sound of that collapse rang in my ears. I heard it again in the Spring of 2008 and the subprime debacle. In the thirty years my own career has spanned, there have been sufficient examples to show that things that seem too good to be true usually are.

Is there a personal experience or an observation from your professional life that serves as your internal barometer and has taught you to:

- respect the laws of nature, including the natural tendencies in economics?
- understand how things are designed and how they are intended to behave and if they are being used in some other way, steer clear?
- stay alert to the environment? assess situations for yourself?

SEEING GHOSTS

That public service announcement about the elderly woman and her daughter-in-law awakened a sense of awareness in me that I wish I'd had when my mother was alive. In those days when her hospital bed was set up in our living room and my siblings were helping us take care of her, I know my mother felt loved. She knew we cared. But I will never know if she felt she had sacrificed her dignity when she couldn't maintain her independence. I don't know if she felt that she was a burden to us. She was still the duchess, and she would never have let on. But did I miss a look in her eyes that seemed so obvious to me through the eyes of another all those years later? I would never know.

From the moment I saw my mother's "ghost" I knew that I had to let people know how important it is to consider those feelings of dignity and independence when we speak to clients about long-term care insurance. These are not easy conversations to have among family members, especially if they happen after a need arises. These are the conversations that an insurance professional can feel so good about having.

Like the moment when you see the hidden picture in a Rorschach test, I can never "un-see" what I saw in the PSA. It has transformed the way I view long-term care insurance. I encourage everyone to consider what it might feel like to be left without options when you need care. This is particularly true because it is the rare individual who can ever hope to save enough to afford years of day-to-day care. Most people find themselves trying to unload assets to qualify for state or federal aid, rather than living comfortably as they might while living independently.

We must accept that some of the significance of life will not come to us in the moment it occurs, but later on as we consider it from a distance.

Think back to some of the significant people in your life (grandparents, parents, spouses) when they faced life changing situations—or when they may face those situations in the future.

- **Try to view each situation from the perspective of those who may not have a voice in their situation. List some of the emotions or considerations they may have (or had).**
- **Think about the human benefits our products deliver beyond the financial benefit: dignity, independence, and peace of mind. Imagine the impact those individuals would feel from experiencing those benefits.**

THINKING BEYOND YOURSELF

I think the person who takes a job in order to live—that is to say, for the money—has turned himself into a slave.

—Joseph Campbell

For most people, it is difficult to sit down face-to-face with someone and convince them to do something if all you have in mind is your own personal gain. I talked about the importance of thinking beyond yourself when you consider what motivates you. This applies in many situations and professions. But people who work in insurance and related products—whether they use a financial planning model or simply establish relationships with clients and help them choose what they need piecemeal—can benefit the most by acknowledging how much your work can do for other people.

You have to bring the full weight of your emotional intelligence to bear as you reassess your motivating factors. Considering others isn't a function of calculations or clinical data. Truly considering others means considering how their lives, or the lives of those they care about, can be sustained or improved through the peace of mind you can bring to them.

Cast your net wide. There are very few people who are in such a safe financial position that you couldn't add some benefit to their lives. Think of the people you know personally, those you know tangentially, those you may not know, but who live and work in your community. See these people through new eyes.

Most people don't have someone watching out for their interests. The pensions and other ironclad benefit plans their grandparents benefited from are not available to them. You have the opportunity to help them restore some security and peace of mind. You can do this when you put their needs first and rely on your expertise.

When you are coming from a stance of fairness, with a goal of being the advocate for the families and business partners of your clients, you can bring a positive, confident attitude to your conversations.

SO, GET INSPIRED

One way to think beyond yourself is to get inspired! A lot of people mistake me for a motivational speaker, but how could I possibly motivate you? Look at the profession you've chosen. You talk to people about things they don't want to talk about and they certainly don't want to see you. Then if they *do* see you, they don't want to buy what you're selling. So that takes plenty of motivation.

The problem with motivation, however, is that you have to drive it. I would submit that sometimes this business can subject you to so much negativity and rejection that motivation alone is not enough to sustain you. I think what you need to do is to get inspired. The beauty of inspiration is that it drives you.

Inspiration is made up of two components: one is your purpose, and the second is making a commitment to your purpose. And so, what is your purpose? You have to recognize that you do something very significant—you could be the most important person in someone's life, a family continues or a business continues or a legacy is spawned for generations by your activities. You've got to not only know it, you've got to believe it and feel it.

Your unique purpose is to make certain that the money outlives the people. If you buy into this definition of your purpose you have to use protection products in your practice because you have to insure against what can go wrong and to gain the luxury to invest for what can go right. The reality of this world is some people die too soon, many people outlive their money, and sometimes people get sick.

Next is your value proposition. The value of the advice you provide and the products you sell are worth far more than what your clients pay for them. Price is only an issue in the absence of value, so let's explore your value. You provide peace of mind when people die prematurely. You can provide people with a worry-free retirement, with an income they can't outlive, so they can maintain their independence. You can protect that income if they get sick so that they maintain their dignity. And finally, you provide legacy when they die.

You tell me if that's not living a significant life, or that's not enough to inspire you. As I said before, it's not enough to know this. You have to believe it, because if you believe it, you will be believed. Your beliefs drive your behavior. A lot of you have very lofty goals and you might desire to achieve them. But if your goals are not in sync with your beliefs, ultimately your behavior will always manifest your beliefs.

And if you are not convinced that you live a significant life, a life of service to others, then you can be victimized by something nobody in this business talks about—low self-esteem. Carter Woodson said that if you can determine how a man thinks, you don't have to worry about what he will do. If someone has an opinion of inferiority, you don't have to compel him to take an inferior position, because he'll get there all by himself.

If you can make someone feel like an outcast, you don't have to tell her to go out the back door; she will get up and go there for herself. And if there is no back door, her very nature will insist on one. How you feel about yourself is very important because all chronic production issues are behavioral. A way to combat negative self-image is to create a cultural environment that celebrates the good that you do. I don't mean to be the industry chaplain, but it is my belief that you need to be inspired by contemplating the positive impact you have on others. It is this inspiration on top of your motivation that will sustain you through the negativity, rejection, and periodic bouts of low self-esteem.

So how do you become inspired? Create a personal culture and insist that your agency create an organizational culture that celebrates the positive impact you have on others. Do whatever it takes to create a culture that reminds you of the good that you do because culture manages when management's not there. You'll need a positive culture to deal with the changes that are coming. Believe in change but never change what you believe.

Speaking about change, it is important to note that not all the coming changes will be negative. I'm sure many of you have heard of Dan Sullivan, the founder of the Strategic Coach® program that serves entrepreneurs, many of them in the financial services area. He just wrote: *The Good That Financial Advisors Do.* And check out this quote: "Being a financial advisor to upwardly mobile individuals in the 21st century is one of the most important roles in our society."

Now that should make you feel pretty good because here is the bigger paradigm that is emerging. The cultural, governmental, and corporate safety nets that people once enjoyed are in jeopardy. In 2011, we're seeing riots in the U.K.; we are seeing riots in Wisconsin and in Greece; and we are seeing riots in France. In France they want to shift the retirement age from 60 to 62. Now, I have a retirement date—it's two weeks before I die.

But that's the trap. These people cannot wait to retire. They might have been enriched, but they are certainly not fulfilled. If you really love what you do, why would you want to retire? If you are unfulfilled and miserable while you're working at 60, what do you think you will be when you're retired at age 62? The same unfulfilled and miserable person in retirement. In life it's not what you get, it's what you become. And as Billy Joel says, "It doesn't matter where you are because you wake up with yourself." The other benefit that our business provides is the ability to be able to do something that's significant and life sustaining. It's not enough to have a job that enriches you; it also has to fulfill you. And it's also important that you follow your true calling in terms of helping people and not just taking a job to pay your bills.

Now having said that, we all recognize that people are living a lot longer. There are no more safety nets. They are going to need someone in financial services—someone like you—to make it. And I think the way our profession will be perceived will be dramatically different. Societies are going to figure out it's cheaper to have financial professionals helping individuals than giving unfunded pensions for someone who is going to live another 30 years in retirement.

Once you believe you do something significant, it's time to take action. Positive thinking doesn't always lead to positive action, but positive action ALWAYS leads to positive thinking. Let me ask a question first: what is the worst part of this business that you dread the most? Nine out of ten in financial services say "asking a stranger to see me and the possibility of rejection." So if we really believe that we have a significant purpose, then we have to make a commitment to that significant purpose. Here's my suggestion: take that number one fear head on.

Make a commitment to ask X number of people a day to see you. That's an actual "ask," not a dial, whether you call them on the phone or see them in person. Because if the market implodes, the big case falls through, some one was mean to you—if you made your commitment that you have asked 7, or 6, or 5, or 4, or in some instances it could be one person to see you, then you've had a successful day. Now if you haven't done this in a while, start off with a reasonable goal. Maybe it's two people a day and then watch your behavior of avoidance take over. You'll be driven to read about some new marketing ideas that you will never use or read the new underwriting manual or you cannot wait to take your continuing education class—anything but facing rejection. But to me this isn't just a process or exercise, it's a reaffirmation of faith—faith that you do something worthwhile.

Saint Augustine said: "...faith is believing in what you can't see, and when you have faith, you can begin to see what you believe." I am not trying to get religious with you, but I do think there is a spiritual side to the business. That's why you have to be solid and have a significant purpose, because it will help drive you to face your fears and make those calls.

The other paradigm this process facilitates is that you are managing to your effort and not to your results. You don't control your results. You cannot control whether someone will see you or whether someone will buy from you. You cannot control underwriting decisions or the stock market or interest rates. The only thing you can control is your effort. To reiterate, if your goal was to ask three people today and you received three no's, you had a successful day. Even Ghandi said that true satisfaction does not come in the achievement, but in the effort. Total effort is total victory. So the idea is to manage what you control, which is your effort. The more you prospect, the better you feel and the more it reaffirms your significant purpose. This is how you can move yourself from motivation to inspiration.

There are three types of people in this world:

1. People who listen to your advice;
2. People who don't listen to your advice; and
3. People who have never heard your advice.

Your job is to keep the people who listen to your advice. Get rid of the people who don't listen to your advice. Approach the people who have never heard your advice, and turn them into people who listen to your advice.

At MetLife, I instituted the daily contact commitment in the latter part of 2007 and, low and behold, in 2010 my mentor, Nick Murray, published a book called *The Game of Numbers*. At one of his seminars, he was amazed to learn that his followers—major financial planning types—had stopped prospecting! He never considered writing a prospecting book because he thought his clientele were beyond it. Looks like we all need to go back to the basics.

Try these exercises:

Make four lists of people you can put into circles of consideration:

1. close friends and relatives
2. acquaintances
3. colleagues in organizations
4. others in your community (business owners, officials, professionals)

Personalize the considerations for each person on your list:

- work situation
- family situation
- life stage
- special circumstances

Think about how you can help address those considerations.

Incorporate them into your daily contact commitment list.

One last point I want to make is that much emphasis is placed on goal setting and rightfully so. Goals are important, but as I said, they have to sync with your beliefs. Goals are the *what,* and technique/knowledge/skills are the *how*. But believing in your purpose that you live a significant life in the service of others is the *why*—why you would practice this profession. The *why* in my judgment needs to transcend beyond your own personal needs. The more global your recognition of *why* leads to greater inspiration which gives you the courage to practice the *how* of the daily contact commitment which reinforces that you do this, and that process will give you the *what* you seek.

Where did you learn your relationship skills?

What motivates you?

What makes you feel great at the end of a work day or the
end of a conversation with a client?

V.

Your Life of Significance

A hero is someone who has given his or her life to something bigger than oneself.

—Joseph Campbell

"Hero" may seem like a big word, but in my presentations, I know I am speaking to heroes every day. I am writing this book for you because you are a hero, too. We have captured hundreds of interviews with heroes who, just by doing their jobs, have changed lives and influenced generations to come. Advocating for a family's financial well-being is heroic because, using Joseph Campbell's definition, it is doing "something bigger than oneself." This is what you have chosen to do. By ensuring that individuals can protect their assets and their personal dignity, and by helping them to build a meaningful legacy, you will build your own legacy as well—one of quiet, heroic significance.

I would not have written this book if I did not believe that everyone can live a life of significance. Many people lead such lives, and never realize the impact they've had on those around them—and on generations yet to come. There are probably just as many people who miss the opportunity to live their lives as significantly as possible because they are out of touch with the signals around them and practices that would help them be more in tune with those signals. Few professions offer the potential to establish such a legacy of significance.

Living a life of significance begins with impact that you can have on the lives of your clients. I can think of no other profession that can provide clients with protection, independence, dignity and legacy. *Living a Life of Significance* isn't just my story—it's YOUR story too!

If nothing else, when you finish reading this book, I want you to be proud and enthusiastic about what you do. It may help if you make some comparisons with professions that are commonly held in some esteem. Consider physicians—they always fail because everyone dies. The help you provide will live on generation after generation through—as Chief Seattle eloquently puts it—the web of life.

A life of significance focuses on the protection of others—something bigger than oneself, the preservation of human dignity—and ultimately it is a life that builds a meaningful legacy of your own. At the beginning of this book, I said not every journey looks the same. At the same time, every journey has a story to tell. From experience, I can offer the following suggestions:

- Question early and often.
- Exercise both sides of your brain.
- Practice the Fairness Doctrine—consider the benefits of considering others.
- Be disciplined—make a daily contact commitment.
- Create celebratory culture.
- Make a commitment—both to your clients and prospecting.
- Trust that you can live a life of significance from where you are right now.

QUESTION EARLY AND OFTEN

Throughout this book, I have encouraged you to question things around you and inside yourself as well. The types of questions we've included in the margins and continued in this chapter are intended to keep your sense sharpened and to better equip you to recognize and respond to situations for yourself and for the clients you serve. Consider this analogy:

In New York, building maintenance is a huge business. One facet of this business involves a meticulous process of tapping on the bricks or stones of a building's façade to insure that each one is solidly in place. If you don't tap the stones, you run the risk that one will come loose and fall onto a busy sidewalk below. The risk is greater if the loose stone is a keystone and a structural collapse might occur. Tapping away at your own façade can ensure that your foundations are strong.

Questions are the way to sound out the potential weaknesses in your self-understanding or your knowledge of your surroundings. Remember, you are in good

74

company when you question something about your life everyday. If you question a little something everyday, you may avoid the day when you find you are very far from where you intended to be.

This means that you should stay awake to the world around you and the world inside you. Make sure that you have an idea where you are and how you fit into the situation. As an insurance professional, you will often find yourself viewing a situation a bit differently than someone else might. For example, when you go to a barbecue or a picnic with friends and family, you may see kids there who wouldn't be there if one or the other of their parents was unable to bring them. Other people might shake off that realization as a maudlin distraction. But unlike other people, you have it in your power to help someone potentially avoid that situation.

Your first step in this process may be to give yourself permission to entertain questions about your own life, your choices, or your career path. If you are comfortable with questions, you have already stepped off of square one.

If you need a bit more encouragement to start questioning, you can review the stories shared in earlier chapters and read the vignettes to follow.

Paris Lewis, a financial advisor, questioned whether a client had the right coverage.

When he first met with this client (let's call him Jim), Paris knew he wasn't Jim's first insurance agent. Jim had a 30-year-old policy already in force. Paris questioned in his own mind from that very first meeting whether this policy was sufficient for Jim. But he let Jim set the pace. Jim went slowly at first, asking simply for a beneficiary change. Paris handled it quickly and efficiently. Jim asked him to handle a few more administrative details. Before long, Jim asked Paris to become his financial advisor, and shared his full financial situation with this professional he had come to trust. Paris revisited Jim's life insurance coverage and reviewed other protection and investment options available to his client.

A few years later, Jim called Paris and asked him to stop by, "as a friend, not a financial advisor." Jim then revealed that he had been diagnosed with Lou Gehrig's disease, a progressive, incurable, ultimately fatal condition.

Paris found his mind racing. Had he considered everything his friend would need to protect his income? To continue a life with dignity and independence? And to leave a legacy for his family? Thankfully, Paris could answer, "Yes." Paris continues to serve Jim's family—his children, widow, siblings, and now his grandchildren—as a trusted financial advisor. To them, Paris is a hero.

Lonnie Colson, a financial advisor, questioned a client's assessment of his own needs.

Lonnie's client—we'll call him Frank—came to Lonnie knowing exactly what he needed. Or so he thought. Frank was thirty years old, with a wife and two young boys. They had just purchased a home, and Frank wanted mortgage insurance. Lonnie questioned the narrowness of Frank's request. He ran a full analysis and spoke to Frank honestly about his family's income and educational needs as deserving of as much consideration as his house payments if anything happened to him. Frank agreed that he had missed the big picture until Lonnie put things in perspective from his family's point of view.

Two months later, Frank's two sons ran out to meet Lonnie as he came up their front walk. In that way that only children can, they confided, "You know, our Daddy isn't coming home anymore." Lonnie did know. He was there to deliver the benefit check to Frank's widow. Frank had been killed in a car accident earlier that week.

Maybe the polite thing for Lonnie to have done two months earlier would have been to nod and tell Frank that insurance to cover his mortgage was a great idea. Maybe it would have made Frank feel smart for "knowing" what he needed. But it wouldn't have protected his family. Lonnie knew that his job was to protect that family, not fill an order like a fast-food pickup window. Lonnie knew the significance of considering the big picture, speaking for those who couldn't speak for themselves—Frank's sons—and helping his clients to see what they really need. Those two boys went straight to college from the home that their father made sure they would not lose when he died, and their education was paid for as well.

As you can tell from these stories, I am not promoting a particular sales approach. Each of these individuals built a relationship in a different way. The point is that they built a relationship. As a result, both their clients' lives and their own lives were enriched.

If you are ready to consider some of the important questions in your own life, you can start with these:

1. **What situations challenge you most? (examples: cold calls, closing, public speaking)**

2. **What situations have been the most satisfying for you?**

3. **What inspired you to pursue the field of insurance?**

4. **Do you have any questions that you didn't have when you started reading this book?**

5. **What would a life of significance look like to you? (It may help to think of people you consider to have lived or be living these kinds of lives.)**

As you work through these questions, you may find that they lead to other questions. That would actually be an excellent outcome. You might want to consider an ongoing practice of revisiting these questions.

THE MOST IMPORTANT QUESTION

There is no more important question than whether the recommendation you make to a client is the one that you consider to be the best choice for that client. As a seasoned professional, I can tell you that you will have greater and more meaningful success when you operate ethically than when you follow any other formula. This is not merely a philosophical position. It has real tangible financial implications.

A 2006 securities industry study found that firms in the securities industry are spending 13.1% of net revenue on compliance-related activities. As an industry, these firms are spending at least $25.5 billion a year on compliance-related activities. Regulatory and legislative mandates on compliance-related spending resulted in major increases for 92.1% of the firms surveyed. These same mandates translated to an increase in the time devoted to compliance since 2002 for 97.2% of the firms surveyed. Average capital expenditures per firm on compliance is $3.9 million dollars, which represents an average increase of 366.1% since 2002.[3]

These trends have an important connection to living a life of significance because compliance is directly related to ethical selling and nothing is more paramount in the financial industry than maintaining client confidence and abiding within the regulatory and legislative mandates established to protect consumers. Living a life of significance is one of ethical behavior. As companies continue to devote an enormous amount of time, money and attention to compliance, they will place ever greater value on the financial professionals who continually do "the right thing" for their clients. Companies understand that when it comes to compliance, an ounce of prevention is worth a pound of cure.

The heart of ethical selling is understanding that we don't just sell products—we advocate for our clients and those who depend upon them. This moral obligation can differentiate you from purely profit-motivated competitors in some ways you might not predict. It can actually provide a distinctly sustainable advantage as over time your solutions will bear out the message you use to sell them.

EXERCISE BOTH SIDES OF YOUR BRAIN

In the financial services industry, the most valuable resource producers have is their ability to connect with people, and that means understanding the difference between left-brain and right-brain concepts:

- The left brain thinks; the right brain feels.
- The left brain communicates; the right brain connects.
- The left brain knows; the right brain believes.

Daniel Pink alerts us in his book, "A Whole New Mind," that intuition should not be underestimated in any profession. It is not a matter of intellect over emotion, but a combination of emotional and rational intelligence that positions people for success. In the business of insurance, I would assert that emotional intelligence is a core competency.

---

3. "The Cost of Compliance in the US Securities Industry," Survey Report, Securities Industry Association, February 2006.

It may also be the key to regaining a sense of self-worth and a real enthusiasm for the valuable service you provide.

Science and sociology agree that you should value both your intelligence and your intuition. Now economists are following suit. In the insurance business, you will want to respect both of these attributes in your clients as well.

One agent's story can serve as a reminder that you want to approach your contacts with their best interest in mind and not your own. There are times when you may be too close to a situation to realize you aren't seeing the person's needs clearly. Read Mike's story to see what I mean.

Measuring Success (Mike Amine's Story)

As a young man, starting out fresh in this business, I was always measuring my own success. We have so many ways to do that. There are awards, achievements, all types of recognition to strive for, and these are all worthy goals. I remember that hitting those targets loomed large in my mind on the day that I went to my parents' house to talk to my dad about a policy on his life. I was very clear that he needed the protection in place to ensure that my mom would be taken care of if anything happened to him. My dad absolutely agreed.

As we were working out the details around the kitchen table, my mom said, "Mike, I'd like you to write a policy for me, too. I want to have life insurance." It was so sweet. But I said, "No, Mom. You don't need life insurance. Nothing's ever going to happen to you." We laughed. And she smiled at me and let it go.

My wife and I were on vacation the next summer when my brother called. "I've got some bad news," he said. "Mom's been diagnosed with ovarian cancer." I literally dropped the phone. My wife had to pick it up and finish the conversation. She told me as gently as she could that things did not look good. Within a year, my mother died from that cancer.

We never spoke about it. But I knew that I had taken away her chance to leave the legacy she wanted to leave. If I had only listened to Mom…. She taught me an invaluable lesson. You see, in my mind, I didn't need to sell my mom a policy that day a few years earlier. I was on track to do the level of business I needed to achieve the

79

success I was looking for that year. I didn't need that extra premium. No. *She* needed it. And I was so focused on my own goals that I denied it to her.

I measure success differently now. I hear my mother's voice loud and clear. Awards are great, but they come second to the important part of this business. What we do is immeasurably significant. We give people that chance to leave a legacy, to live with dignity, to give something to their loved ones at the most difficult time they will face. Because I didn't listen to my mother, her voice echoes in my ear, and I will never make that mistake again. I hear you, Mom.

TRUST THAT YOU CAN HAVE A JOURNEY OF SIGNIFICANCE FROM WHERE YOU ARE RIGHT NOW

Is the system going to flatten you out and deny you your humanity, or are you going to be able to make use of the system to the attainment of human purposes?

—Joseph Campbell

I will reiterate my belief that everyone can live a life of significance. By this point in the book, you may be thinking that the profession you are in can lead you toward that life of significance. I will say that I cannot think of many professions, especially in the financial services arena, that offer such an opportunity to change lives and influence future generations in a way that will ensure a meaningful legacy.

As you'll recall, I have stayed on course with my internal compass in many ways. I have changed jobs, and I have changed companies in some cases. Other times, I found a way to stay in the same company and maintain my course, working to change things from within. I would encourage you to understand that you don't have to leave your job or change your profession to achieve a life of significance. In fact, if you are in the insurance business, I am confident that you can live such a life. In fact, you probably already do.

As our business grows and changes, our reach has become increasingly global. Our ability to touch lives now extends across all seven continents. The story of one American agent and her Chinese client gives a view of that worldwide connection and its immeasurable value to clients around the globe.

Last Wish

The story of Ying Ling Zhang is one that shows how service can reach around the globe and how personally clients come to value those who help them make the right decisions in life. Ying Ling tells of a client who bought a policy at the beginning of one summer and was diagnosed with cervical cancer the following June. She called Ying Ling to tell her of her first surgery and soon called to say that she had not much time left to live and wanted to go home to China to be with her aging mother.

Ying Ling assured her that everything would be taken care of here at home. She then set the necessary process in motion to ensure that although her client's treatments were nearly $1,000 per day, the checks would arrive to cover her care.

As she neared the end of her life, Ying Ling's client asked her husband to call Ying Ling and thank her. Although she could no longer speak, she wanted Ying Ling to know that she was "the person I want to thank most on earth. I will pray for her from heaven."

As Ying Ling tells this incredibly moving story, her humility is striking. "It was she [meaning her client] who made the right decision," she says quietly. Of course, this is true; none of us can force a client to make a decision. But Ying Ling clearly made a tremendous difference in her client's life—and ultimately in her quality of life, her independence to travel thousands of miles for her final days, and the dignity of dying in her own way. Ying Ling's is a life of significance on a global scale.

At this point, I'd like to talk a bit about the self-esteem issue. I am an advocate for a healthy sense of self-esteem. When you understand the value of what you can do for your clients, and you focus on how that value can make a difference for them, you can break down the negative stereotypes and let your best self come through. When you understand your role as advocate, you will strike a healthy balance in your own self-image.

Answer these questions from the Rosenberg self-esteem test to assess where you fall on the self-esteem spectrum (on a scale of 1 to 5, where 5 is the highest) and build a plan to strike a balance:

1. On the whole, I am satisfied with myself.

2. At times, I think I am no good at all.

3. I feel that I have a number of good qualities.

4. I am able to do things as well as most other people.

5. I feel I do not have much to be proud of.

6. I certainly feel useless at times.

7. I feel that I'm a person of worth, at least on an equal plane with others.

8. I wish I could have more respect for myself.

9. All in all, I am inclined to feel that I am a failure.

10. I take a positive attitude toward myself.

Add the scores for answers 1, 3, 4, 7, and 10. Then subtract the scores for 2, 5, 6, 8 and 9 from the total. An overall score below 15 indicates low self-esteem.

It's important to remember that all the hard work, intelligence, and emotional commitment in the world cannot guarantee that every client will make the best decisions. Rejection is a common occurrence in our business. There will always be clients who cannot "get out of their own way." In those situations, we can learn new lessons to apply another time, but we cannot fall into the trap of allowing our own self-esteem to be tied to the results.

One such story was shared with us by Roland Basinski.

I had a client who was about to retire. He called me up to say that he was letting his whole life policies lapse. He just couldn't see his way clear to keep up the premiums. These policies totaled $500,000. I took the opportunity to get together with my client and talk about the importance of maintaining that coverage, especially since Social Security was the only other buffer he and his wife had. He was immovable on the topic. All he could think of was the money going out.

Sure enough, he let the policies lapse. Soon afterward he died, leaving his wife only the Social Security to live on. I was heartbroken, but I knew that I had done my best to convince him to keep the policies current.

The only thing I could take away from this experience is a greater awareness that I should touch base with my clients—even when they're covered and I think they're doing fine. If I had asked him about this ten years earlier, maybe I could have helped him avoid this panicked reaction. As it is, I have to remind myself, it was his decision. Hopefully, I'll help my other clients get out in front of their retirement choices.

PERSONAL JOURNEY

You each have your own personal journey as a financial professional and as a person. Seldom does a profession allow you success in both. As I have revealed in this book, the mother-in-law PSA that I saw in 1999 had me think about the potential impact life insurance would have had on my family. Up until then, I never talked about my personal situation. I fell into the trap of separating who I was from what I did. This absence of balance is endemic in the West and leads to the situations we see in France, where people cannot wait to retire.

I spoke of my anger being expressed at MDRT in 2004 on the main platform. For the first time, I personalized the business I had been in for thirty years. I shared how the Joseph Campbell connection to Chief Seattle revealed a culture and a way of thinking that did not compartmentalize life. Rather it was in harmony, that WHAT you do and WHO you are as one. That helped, but it did not complete the transformation.

In 2006, when I was 54 years old, two years after the 2004 MDRT presentation, I found myself at a meeting in the home office. One of the participants was complaining about my abruptness, or according to this person, my unwillingness to listen to others. I had heard this feedback in the past and while I did not agree with all of it, I did feel I needed to listen. So I said to myself, why does this appear to be a reoccurring theme? Why do some people react to me like this? Have you ever gone into a thought process where you mind takes off into ever deeper subjects? Within nanoseconds, my mind was asking, how did I get into this business? Why is it I am speaking to tens of thousands of people around the world every year? How did it happen? The answer came to me in an instant.

I feel that I have been directed (unbeknownst to me) by my mother to get to where I am today. As Joseph Campbell would say, the way I "follow my bliss" is to talk to the thousands who can save the millions from a fate like the one she had to endure.

For the first time in my life, WHO I was and WHAT I did, were in harmony. I understood my purpose. My life had meaning. In life it is not the pain of the journey, but the rapture of the revelation. You all have your personal journeys and remember the research I did that everyone dies? Well, that means you, too.

So how will you live your life?

One final note: Let me tell you the best thing about my transformation. I remember that my mother always wanted to go home to Ireland, but she never made it. In 2006, my MDRT buddy, Brendan Glennon invited me to speak at the MDRT meeting in Dublin. I told her story and showed her image ...I took my mother home.

Nothing that is worth doing can be achieved in a lifetime; therefore we must be saved by hope.

Nothing which is true or beautiful or good makes complete sense in any immediate context of history;

Therefore we must be saved by Faith.

Nothing we do, however virtuous, can be accomplished alone;

Therefore we are saved by Love.

—Adapted from the poem written by Reinhold Niebuhr

Buy Your Copy Today and Accelerate Your Own Journey to Significance

Living a Life of Significance is industry legend Joe Jordan's masterpiece of inspiration, personal reflection, and motivation. This amazing new book is sure to impact your connection to this incredible profession and every customer you serve.

Shipping Information

First Name _____ Last Name _____

Company _____

Address _____

City _____ State _____ Zip Code _____

Phone _____ Email _____

Credit Card Billing Information

Shipping Address and Credit Card Billing Address are the same

First Name _____ Last Name _____

Company _____

Address _____

City _____ State _____ Zip Code _____

Phone _____ Email _____

$14.99 each! *(Shipping and price vary based on quantity)*

Quantity	Book Price	S&H	Quantity	Book Price	S&H
1 - 9	$14.99	$6.00	100 - 249	$10.50	$50.00
10 - 24	$12.50	$12.00	250 - 499	$10.50	$100.00
25 - 99	$10.50	$25.00	500 + Books	$9.00	No S&H

Quantity_____ Shipping $_____ Total $_____

❏ Enclosed is a check payable to **The American College**

Please mail to: Textbook Department
The American College
270 S. Bryn Mawr Ave.
Bryn Mawr, PA 19010

Please charge my: ❏ VISA ❏ MasterCard
❏ Discover ❏ American Express

Card Number_____ Exp._____

Signature _____

Order Online at TheAmericanCollege.edu/Significance or fax this form to 610-526-1545

Questions, please call 610-526-1350 or email Textbooks@TheAmericanCollege.edu